Watsons Bay
17th Feb. '96

Hello, on this lovely morning
in Sydney town. Sydney harbour
sparkling in the sunshine all
the way to our beautiful city
on the harbour, and the Opera
House.
"All things bright and beautiful"
after the recent precious rains
of Summer. Take time off to
smell the flowers and look at
the trees.   Cheers, happy days
to you and yours and may all
your dreams come true.
          Sinc
     Alice & Jean Doyle
     Founders of Doyles

DOYLE'S
FISH COOKBOOK

April, 1996

Dear Joe & Jen,

    Hope you will cook many
    splendid meals with this book!

Wishing you lots of luck in your new
    home. We look forward to many
    more wonderful meals.......

We are sure that the friendship we
have developed in Hong Kong will
continue for many many many year to
come.

    All our Love
    Howard and
       Lisa

My grandfather's first home at Vaucluse Bay,
on land belonging to William Charles Wentworth.
Many fishermen lived in this hut over the years.

DOYLE'S
FISH COOKBOOK
Alice Doyle

Angus&Robertson
An imprint of HarperCollins*Publishers*

The beautiful waterfront at Watson's Bay, before the turn of the century.

To my dear sister Flo
and
to everyone connected with the seafood business

I know exactly what it's like to be "the lady from the fish shop". So here's to the fish folk — all those folk who depend on fish for a living. I know just how you all feel at times. We live with it, handle it, catch it, clean it, sell it, explain the species, answer the constant question "Is it fresh?". (As if we would say "No"!) It's worse when you have a restaurant. With all the sea around you, the customers can't understand why John Dory is not on today, or there are no lobsters. "But why?" they ask, after I explain about seasonal shortages and huge seas. "The Harbour seems so calm."

Congratulations especially to the fish cleaners, who do such a good job in preparing the fish for people to cook. You try to live down that unmistakable smell of fish when you meet your mates at the local for a schooner or two after a day's hard work, and then you head for home for a hot shower and a clean up, knowing you have to leave those smelly old gumboots outside the back door and your clothes in the laundry. You don't dare go in the house first. Mum and the family will see to that.

I know all about that smell — how many times do we all wish we were in the chemists' line of business, and smelling like it. But, folks, we're stuck with it! And after all, nowadays seafood is luxury food, and a couple of decent crayfish with a mud crab thrown in are more expensive than a small-sized bottle of Joy — the world's most expensive perfume.

The author's royalties from the sale of this book
are paid to the City Night Refuge section of the
Sydney City Mission.

Angus&Robertson
An imprint of HarperCollins*Publishers*, Australia

First published in Australia by Angus & Robertson Publishers in 1979
Reprinted in 1980, 1982, 1983, 1984
Second edition 1986
Reprinted in 1986, 1987, 1988, 1989
This edition 1989
Reprinted in 1990, 1992, 1993, 1995

HarperCollins*Publishers*
25 Ryde Road, Pymble, Sydney, NSW 2073, Australia
31 View Road, Glenfield, Auckland 10, New Zealand
77-85 Fulham Palace Road, London W6 8JB, United Kingdom
Hazelton Lanes, 55 Avenue Road, Suite 2900, Toronto, Ontario M5R 3L2
and 1995 Markham Road, Scarborough, Ontario M1B 5M8, Canada
10 East 53rd Street, New York NY 10032, USA

National Library of Australia Cataloguing-in-Publication data:

Doyle, Alice.
Doyle's fish cookbook
3rd edition.

Includes index.
ISBN 0 207 16022 8.
I. Cookery (Fish) 2. Cookery (Seafood). I. Title.

641.6'92

Cover illustration by Skye Rogers
Typeset in 10 pt Baskerville by Midland Typesetters, Maryborough
Printed in Singapore

18 17 16 15   95 96 97 98

Acknowledgments

My thanks to all those people who helped me put this book together, especially Dr Don Francois, former Director of Fisheries, New South Wales State Fisheries, the late Mr Mark Joseph, former Chairman of the New South Wales Fish Marketing Authority, Mr Graham Jones, the Authority's former General Manager, and the Sydney Fish Marketing Authority, Pyrmont, which kindly supplied the information on buying and keeping fish at the back of the book. Thank you, George Sautelle, for supplying some of the marvellous pictures of old Watson's Bay. Thank you, dear Louise Lendrum, who helped me with my typing and battled with my handwriting.

Thanks, too, to all those Australian hosts and hostesses who contributed their favourite recipes—especially my friend and one-time hotel chef George Heydon. But most of all, thanks to my old Watson's Bay friends, my husband and my family, who encouraged me and helped me in this, as they have in so many other things all our lives together.

For their help in preparing this third edition, a very special thank you to my granddaughter Deborah Irvine, who really read my thoughts, and, once again, to my husband (of fifty-seven years), Jack, who ate lots of fish and chips brought home from the restaurant to save me cooking and let me get on with this new edition. Thanks also to Accoutrement (Castlecrag, Chatswood and Mosman) for supplying many of the accessories used in the colour photographs.

Most of the black and white photographs in this book are of old Watson's Bay, taken around the turn of the century.

Doyle's on the Beach today.

Contents

The battleship SS Sydney *passing by Green Point, Watson's Bay, in 1920. On the left are the old Watson's Bay Baths, with their high diving tower, which my father leased from the Vaucluse (now the Woollahra) Council in 1915 and ran for ten years. On the right is the old waiting shed at Watson's Bay wharf. Note, too, the big Moreton Bay fig tree and the kiosk with its lattice verandah, where penny ice-creams tasted like the heaven our Sunday school teachers kept telling us about.*

The Harvest from the Sea

Australia is noted all over the world for its fabulous foods from the sea. When I think of the oceans surrounding our continent, and especially when I sail on our beautiful Pacific, I think of all that lives under that azure blue water. No wonder you don't have to cook your fish for long — they don't develop any tough muscles; for them swimming is easy work. And, you know, fish aren't so dumb; they eat very well (so if I were you I'd bathe between the flags). The sea is very rich in vitamins, minerals and proteins, and fish collect all these valuable nutrients when they eat. When we eat them, we benefit from their collection.

The delicate flavour of fish and shellfish, plus their low kilojoule, high energy content, make dieting with seafood a natural. Just one serving provides nearly all the protein needed each day to help build and repair body tissue. In addition to being rich in vitamins and minerals, seafoods are low in fats and high in "fill-ability".

Weather and seasons play a big part in our supply of seafoods. At times your favourite species of fish or shellfish becomes very scarce and expensive, though often no more expensive than the better cuts of meat. There are also seasons when some kinds of fish become very plentiful — fish like mullet and gemfish, for example, at which some people — "fish snobs" — turn up their noses. But don't be put off these fish, because so many delicious dishes can be made using them. Have a look at some of my recipes in this book.

New Australians from all over the world have introduced us old Australians to lots of seafoods that once we would not have thought of eating. Once I could not walk on the rocks bounding the sea around our area because the oysters, sea eggs, pippies and other shellfish would cut my feet to pieces when I went barefoot (what other way?). And those ockies (octopus) I would find in crevices and old tins I'd just lift up on a stick and throw back into the water. There were always dozens of squid hanging around your fishing line, and you couldn't stand catching them because of all that black ink you were certain to be squirted with. Now all these creatures are considered delicacies — and priced like them — and those same rocks are practically smooth. It makes you think. Times change, but fish is now, more than ever, Australia's national food.

I hope this book will help "sell" seafoods — and good health — to you all.

ALICE DOYLE

*Camp Cove, Sydney Harbour. The two-storey building is Sydney's first
Marine Biology Station, and to the right, on Lang's Point, is a monument to
Captain Arthur Phillip's first landing in 1788.*

In Praise of Fish

Seafoods on the average are the most digestible of foods and ideally adapted for bodily assimilation by man. No poor fish ever gets so tough as some of those range steers you run into.

Did you know that man cannot exist for three months in perfect health without the essentials contained in seafoods? Without charging you any more per pound, fishes assimilate these essential chemicals from the sea and you know what you have to pay in the chemist's for substitute drugs.

Fish extract iodine from the sea to prevent you contracting goitre; oysters extract copper from the sea to enrich your bloodstream. Also calcium, phosphorus and iron to keep your bones and flesh intact, even fluorine and arsenic for your fingernails, as well as vitamins you require from A to D.

We cannot divulge all the other benefits you derive, or fishermen would want more for their fish and the Government would impose a tax on food with such high drug content.

You had better rush out right now and buy yourself some fish. Brother! You need it!

from *The Fisheries Newsletter*,
August 1956

Introduction

ABOVE: *The Ozone Refreshment Rooms, 1908. At this time the Ozone was a focal point of Watson's Bay, with its roof garden (reached by stairs from the top dining room) and its outdoor seating at the harbour's edge.*

PREVIOUS PAGE: *Grandma and Grandfather's tea rooms, in the 1880s.*

Introduction

It's very exciting for me to be writing a book, especially a book about fish. When I told my husband and my family about it, they said, "Well, go ahead, Mum—if you don't know about seafood by now after all these years, you may as well give up the game!" I was fortunate enough to have been born in Watson's Bay, Sydney, at a time when lots of professional fishermen lived there. I was brought up with my three sisters and two brothers at that old-fashioned cafe that still sits on the Marine Parade, Watson's Bay, with a tin overhanging roof supported by posts. It used to be called the Ozone Cafe—now it's Doyle's on the Beach. It's not an imposing building by any means. No architect ever drew plans for it. Wilky Schweers, a well-known carpenter and a much loved and respected citizen of the Bay (and, of course, married to one of Mum's relations), worked on it.

We all love the place, and I hope it will stay and be repaired and renewed over the years and that no council or planning scheme will make my family remove it. When the westerly gales are on and the storms whip up a huge sea, I always say a little prayer for the little cafe— and so far so good, because it keeps on being there, intact, when everything's calm again. It was a few years ago that we changed its name to Doyle's on the Beach, to distinguish it from our restaurant on the wharf at Watson's Bay. So many Sydney people from all walks of life visit this beautiful spot, and, of course, many overseas and interstate visitors come to sit on the beachfront to enjoy their lunch, too. The setting is unique, and I am sure it equals in beauty and charm any other waterside eating spot in the world. Gazing up the Harbour to the city of Sydney, watching the huge container ships coming and going and the ferries and small pleasure craft moving around, is fascinating and relaxing.

No wonder our customers often don't want to leave and sit lingering over a cup of coffee until sunset. I think the old restaurant on the beach has such an atmosphere—at times I'm sure it's haunted by my late grandparents and parents. They loved it so, like we all do.

Grandfather and Grandmother Newton opened their first little cafe in a tiny little shop on that same spot on the Watson's Bay promenade in the late 1880s. Ferries, notably the *Bee* and the *Fairy Queen*, used to bring picnic parties to the Bay, so Grandma did a little business at the shop in the fine weather, and Grandfather fished. They had a fuel stove out the back, and they used to cook scones and fry fish and chips for the picknickers. Most of the fuel they used came from the beachfront—driftwood and coke.

Grandfather Newton had a hut on land belonging to the Wentworth Estate in Coolong Road, Vaucluse. He mended his nets there. Grandfather used to take the VIPs of Sydney out fishing, and then he would bring them back to the hut and would make his famous soup with the bones and heads and scraps from some of the fish he'd caught. He'd fry the fillets and serve them with the soup. I still have Grandfather's recipe for that soup, as my mother made it for many years at the restaurant (see page 46). I often wonder how much he charged for those lovely day's outings and that delicious meal he put on afterwards. Of course, I don't know what they drank—no fancy wines, I suppose, like today—but I'm sure Grandfather Newton after a hard (call it hard) day's fishing and sailing with his party would have always made sure there was a hot toddy to warm everybody up and start the old fish yarns off.

3

They reckon my grandfather bent his elbow too much and didn't see all that cheap land known as the Vaucluse Estate being sold all around him, with prices starting at thirty shillings an acre. I don't care about that—what does it matter? He was a good grandfather and was much loved. He enjoyed his life, and the love of the sea was very strong in him, like it is in me. I drive everybody crazy at times admiring sunrise and sunset and the moon on the Harbour and feeding the seagulls. (Seagulls down our way are very choosy nowadays—they won't have bread, but hold out for fish pieces left over from the restaurants. I get into trouble for feeding them because it encourages them on to the boats—I must admit they do make a mess.)

The Smith brothers came and settled in Watson's Bay, and they, along with Grandfather, net fished all the inlets of the Harbour. (There's a photograph of the Smith brothers on pages 118 and 119.) Of course, there were lots of pilots and fishermen living in Watson's Bay, on the water's edge, at that time. By pilots I mean the pilots that used to take the sailing ships up to the port of Sydney. They all tendered for the jobs, and in between waiting for ships to come in lots of them fished and stayed at Camp Cove beach.

The Smith brothers were very hard-working and they looked the part—suntanned and healthy to look at. (When I was a kid, they always reminded me of the label on that well-known Cod Liver Oil mixture. As I write this, I can even taste it! It must have been cheap to buy—everybody had a bottle in the house, do you remember?) You would see the Smith brothers and some of their crew out practically every day. They worked very hard, and seemed to be out in all weathers, even with an easterly gale. Those easterly gales used to cause a big drawback of the water on the beach down in Watson's Bay, and I found them very frightening.

There was always lots of excitement as the nets were pulled in, and the sight always attracted a crowd. You would see two hefty men standing on the beach yards apart, pulling the net gently, and a couple of the crew on the rowing boats standing up, oars working slowly, as the net was hauled in. Sometimes there was a good catch: bream, whiting, silver bream, black bream, sand flathead and always plenty of seaweed. (Really we should eat seaweed, but I can't give you a recipe—I've never sort of fancied it.) In the nets, as well as the fish, there would be lots of exciting odds and ends such as seahorses, sea stars, squid and octopus. There used to be an Italian man down there who would go and buy squid and octopus from the Smiths. I used to screw up my nose at that, in those days, but I have learned differently now . . .

After the haul, the net fishermen had to take up their nets and put them on the rails of the Watson's Bay wharf to dry. Then they'd clean them and pick out all the debris they collected in the sea. (Now, before you rush out and buy a net, you had better ring the Fish Marketing Authority in your state and find out all about the rules and regulations governing net fishing these days. We have to protect our fishing industry, and we don't want to fish out the beaches and harbours by catching fish when they are too small.)

The Smith family lived very near my Grandfather—next door but one, with an old boatshed in between. They had a lovely old weatherboard home with a big verandah that was always draped with nets. They had a little backyard, too, with lots of lemon trees and apricot trees. I'll never forget those trees, especially the apricots. I've never tasted apricots like them since. They needed those lemon trees, because everybody in the district, I'm sure, procured their lemons there for the fish they bought.

In front of the cottage was a lovely old shed—right on Marine Parade, because there was no promenade then—and this old shed was piled up with nets, anchors, kerosene lamps, billy

4

cans, frying pans, old grey blankets, buoys, old, dried-out, curiously-shaped fish and odd-shaped fish backbones marked where sharks had attacked the fish when they were young. There were cats galore, and not one of them with an ounce of spare flesh. They say fish are slimming, and these cats proved it. They were breeding like mad, and of course suckling their kittens, yet they lived entirely on fish. Their coats were smooth and shining, and I remember how they would come over to you, purring with satisfaction, after a feed of fish.

The Smith brothers lived long lives, and Grandmother Smith must have been 100, I think, when she died. She used to help in making and repairing the nets. Most of their diet was fish — I know, because I used to play with the grandchildren, Mary and Maggie Cameron. (We remained lifelong friends.) The brothers used to stay out all night some nights — and Grandfather did, too — looking for schools of fish. I remember old Jack Smith at the age of eighty-five was up a tree on a lookout around Camp Cove, I think it was, and fell down with excitement when he saw a large school of mullet. He broke his leg but, amazingly, completely recovered and after a while was back on light duties down on the beach, repairing nets and so on. I can see him now just gazing up the Harbour, daydreaming a little and puffing on his pipe.

There was always great excitement in Watson's Bay when the salmon season was on — and the mullet season, too. The mullet season here in Watson's Bay was from about March on. After a hot day the Southerly Buster, the big, cool southerly wind, would come, and that was a signal to be on the lookout. The season went right up to Easter. There would be hundreds of fish netted, and the fishermen used to make a pen of netting attached to the rails of the wharf down in the Bay and each day they'd put all the fish they'd caught into this. They'd leave them there till they had a big load, and then trucks from the market would come down and the fish would be brought up to the footpath, shovelled into boxes and taken away. A lot of the salmon went to the fish processors for fish paste. It was exciting to us locals at the time — I suppose now no one would look. Simple but happy days. I think the fishermen received about tuppence a pound for their catch — none of them ever made a fortune, just a living. But they lived long lives and happy lives; they weren't looking for glamour.

My mother was born in Watson's Bay, as my grandfather had been, and as I was. She died at eighty-four after a hard working life, but she loved every moment of it. She wasn't a regular churchgoer, but she and her relatives, along with other early Watson's Bay settlers, raised the money to build St Peter's, the church on the hill. I still have the prayer book that she read nightly. It is nearly in tatters, so I have it tied together with ribbon — such a simple faith, but so loving.

I had a wonderful childhood — well, I think it was wonderful. It was spent amid everything connected with the sea. Plenty of rowing boats on the beach, fish traps, fish nets, sails. I used to have a boat — an old dinghy — and I often wonder how on earth we made it back home sailing from Neilson Park with those stiff nor-easters that blow across Sydney Harbour.

Grandma and Grandfather's little shop was pulled down (or blown down) about 1907. The Ozone Cafe was built on the same spot in 1908. A section of the original little shop still survives as part of the restaurant — we make the entrees there every day.

After the Ozone was built, it was leased out for a while, because my mother and father had started another business at Signal Hill, Watson's Bay, right opposite the signal station, which is about where Belah Gardens is now. I believe they had the first gas stove in Watson's Bay installed there. Next door to the signal station is a gun turret, where one of the largest guns belonging to the Army was housed, and my parents told me later that when it was gun practice time they used to have to take the show window out of the Tea Rooms because the noise the gun made when it was being fired had broken it once before.

Watson's Bay was always a popular place to visit—it was quite an enjoyable trip out by horse buggy or tram from the city. The terminus then was at Signal Hill. Mum was very fond of cooking with that gas stove, and as she was an excellent cook people came back and back. Mum and Dad never made a fortune at the Signal Tea Rooms—just enough to keep the family going, with the help of some fowls and a cow. They used to serve a hot luncheon for two shillings—mostly fish with apple pie to follow. The visitors would then go for a stroll down to Watson's Bay and visit all the beauty spots. When they climbed back up the hill to catch their conveyance to the city, they were quite welcome to call in to Mum and Dad's Tea Rooms again and have some hot scones and a cup of tea—this time nothing to pay, just a friendly gesture, a chance to say "Cheerio till we see you again". You see, they had regulars, and it's good to have regular customers—that's what's kept our family business going for so many years.

Eventually, Mum and Dad went back to the Ozone, and it became a very well-known Sydney eating place. We kids grew up there, helping out in all sorts of ways. Mum and Dad used to do all the cooking, and the customers could have their fish steamed, fried or grilled. With your fish your had mashed potatoes or chips and always, if you wanted it, a dish of oyster sauce as an extra, for a few pence. Of course, the sauce would be made the correct way: if the fish was steamed you'd have the juice out of that to add to your basic white sauce, then the oysters would be added to warm through for a minute or two—mouthwatering!

They presented the fish beautifully, on sizzling hot plates with plenty of parsley and lemon wedges. No side salads in those days—just the fish and potato, perfectly cooked. I always say that even after all these years we can't fry fish and chips as well as Mum did. The batter on the fish in those days was golden like corn, crisp as the thinnest biscuit wafer you can imagine. When a fork was put into the fried fish, the batter practically blew away. All the fish frying was done in pure beef dripping in those days. It had a beautiful smell as it was cooking, and I can remember putting cold dripping on my toast with pepper and salt. It was delicious. (Now, don't make a face. Plenty of people have had a snack like that—but what would my doctor think!) Really, in my opinion there is nothing to beat pure beef dripping for baking or frying, and none of the polyunsaturated oils we use today impart that special flavour to the food.

The Ozone Cafe had two floors. The ground floor was the oyster room, and I can clearly remember its beautiful marble table tops with their wrought iron stands, so many of them, and plenty of flowers in jars all round the room. Each day the lino was freshly polished. Each day, too, pepper and salt shakers and vinegar jars had to be filled up. Every marble table had its own bottle of black sauce (worcestershire sauce), with a serviette tied around the bottle.

The oysters were kept up the back in the fish room. This had a concrete floor and was gauzed in with a wire door. The fish ice chests were kept there. With every order of oysters you had to rush, and I mean rush, up the stairs from the bottom dining room out to the fish room and open the oysters yourself. Just as well we didn't have the crowds to serve that we have nowadays! The wet bags had to be taken off the oysters, and using Grandfather's oyster opener you set to work. It was a wonderful oyster opener—Grandfather made it himself. I never did know what became of it, and nor did Mum. It should have been patented—would have made a fortune for us. Mum always warned us to be careful, with the oysters at ten shillings

TOP: *The tram lines were extended from Signal Hill to Watson's Bay wharf in 1909.*

BOTTOM: *St Peter's Anglican church was consecrated in 1864. At right is the Watson's Bay public school, built in 1877, which my mother, my sisters and brothers, and I all attended.*

a bag, and not to waste them by sticking the knife into them while you were opening them. And, of course, not to eat any ourselves.

The top dining room of our restaurant was very homely, with lovely round tables with white table cloths, each table with an old-fashioned elegant cruet and a little vase of flowers, mostly wildflowers that Grandfather used to get from the bush. I used to gather flannel flowers for the restaurant myself, and red-tipped gum from parks nearby.

The menu at the Ozone was always written freshly every day and placed in a brass container outside the entrance door. I wonder why they bothered—prices didn't fluctuate and the fish was practically the same every day. Of course, mullet predominated when the season was on, and let me tell you now it was popular and really delicious.

Watson's Bay was a very popular place to visit by ferry in those days, as it had been in my grandparents' time. Visitors would catch the ferry from Circular Quay, and on the way to the Bay the ferry would call at Garden Island, then Neilson Park wharf, then it would come round Bottle 'n' Glass (a very pleasant picnic area there). On it would go to Parsley Bay wharf, then pass the suspension bridge across Parsley Bay and continue to Central Wharf, the wharf that brought you up to the Crescent in Vaucluse. A few hundred yards on from Central Wharf was the Watson's Bay wharf. The wharf was very picturesque with its old-fashioned waiting shed. It was a favourite fishing spot for young and old, and there would always be a scurry to pull your line in quickly just as the ferry came pounding in. Gosh, there must have been a lot of big ones got away there.

In summer, people would bring their swimsuits and have a swim in the baths. Not many people swam at Camp Cove or Lady Jane in those days—probably frightened of sharks. We kids used to swim out in front of the restaurant. I guess we were lucky. The old Watson's Bay wharf waiting shed was pulled down, and in its place stand the Sydney Big Game Fishing Association clubrooms. They weigh the sharks and marlin at the weighing platform there. It was a great loss to the local environment when that old shed was taken away, both because it was an historic building and because of its unusual design. Perhaps Urban Transport thought that the ferry would never again come to Watson's Bay, but plans are presently being discussed to have the Manly ferry call here.

Down near the wharf at one time there was a huge old tree, and under this tree the line and net fishermen used to spread their fish out on a table to sell. After you bought it, you either cleaned it yourself or asked the fishermen to do it for you. Fish was fairly plentiful then, and you could buy beautiful big deep-sea flathead, snapper, huge jewfish, bream, garfish and lots of other fish there, including some choice pig fish. Pig fish has beautiful, succulent white flesh, and mostly the fishermen would keep these for themselves, unless you were a special customer. Often the day's catch of fish would be a mixed lot, but it was always worth buying. There were also plenty of mussels and oysters for the taking on the rocks around the Bay and the other Harbour bays. The oysters were small and very strong in flavour but most popular, and many a bottle was collected and raffled at the local hotel over the years.

The Ozone Cafe was closed in the Depression, but as it was my parents' home it remained in the family. Jack and I lived there with our four sons for many years. Then, when my husband returned from the Second World War, I felt I wanted to reopen the business. The New South Wales government had an Army rehabilitation programme which made loans available to ex-servicemen to help them get started again. They refused permission for our loan, saying that

TOP: *Jack and I on the day we reopened my family's old restaurant, the Ozone Cafe, 28 March 1948.*

BOTTOM: *The old ferry waiting shed on the Watson's Bay wharf, around the turn of the century.*

the little old "cafe" was too bad a risk. So Mum came to our rescue with the £60 it took us to equip, and we were in business again. The fish was reasonably plentiful, and we could buy locally. (This is, of course, illegal now.) The fish meal was three shillings and sixpence, with bread and butter, a pot of tea and hot scones and jam thrown in. Mum made the scones and the jam and also her father's famous fish soup.

There were still lots of fishermen living in Watson's Bay then, and Hedley Tinker was still net fishing, taking over from his old relatives, the Smiths. Bill Love was a well-known and very much respected fisherman in the Bay then. He was the late Sam Hordern's boatman on his big game cruiser, and in those days they really caught the big sharks. Then there were the Abbott brothers, Jim Chapman and Jack Farrell—Bay fishermen, who also used a lot of set lines and caught the most beautiful snapper. I used to go down to the boats and buy for the cafe, at the same time admiring these beautiful creatures from the sea. Snapper, to me, are one of the most outstanding fish that swim in our waters, with their beautiful shades of pinks and those clear blue eyes and the shining iridescent scales on their big frames. Some of them as they get older have a big hump on the top part of their spine or backbone—I believe that is a guide to their age. Sounds as if I am describing a beauty competition. Well, they are beauties to us and anyone else that partakes of them.

It was hard work, getting started again. I used to clean fish in the morning out in the garden, and then cook it for the lunchtime crowd. It was always a rush, but it was such a good time, too. The business has grown so now—from one little cafe to four restaurants. It makes you smile to think how the "bad risk" has turned out! I think we've done well because we've always stuck to the one principle that Mum followed in her time: perfect, fresh fish, cooked and served simply, but well—and plenty of it! Our menu still says that there is no charge for an extra portion of fish, if you still happen to be hungry.

One happy part of reopening the restaurant in 1948 was the good wishes of our friends in the Bay, accompanied by the words, "We'll give you a hand very willingly until you can afford to employ staff," and they did. The first weekend in the Easter season, a couple of weeks after we opened, an old friend of my parents, John (Uncle John) Fitzpatrick, who at that time was living at Westmead, came to see us. "I've got my apron with me," he said, "and I'm going to do the washing up on the weekends." And he did—he helped us so much for three years.

John Fitzpatrick had come to Australia as a young man from Dublin in 1907, on the SS *Medic*. (The fare was £17 in those days.) He answered an advertisement my father had put in the *Herald* for a handyman who could milk a cow, tend to the kitchen and help in the Signal Tea Rooms. When my mother opened the door to the handsome young Irishman, complete with Donegal tweeds, cap and cane—and, of course, the voice and charm to match—she had to tell him that she had given the job to another young man earlier in the day. John's reply was: "Here, give him this half-crown, engage me, and you will not be sorry." So that Irish charm brought John Fitzpatrick into our life, and he later married my mother's girlfriend, beautiful Emily Kennedy.

My mother often told me this story of her and Dad's early days, and of how busy they were at the tea rooms when the first American fleet ever to visit Sydney arrived in 1908. People walked out from Sydney to the Gap, if they couldn't get on to one of the early trams, to see the ships come through the Heads and into Sydney Harbour. It must have been quite a night and a day.

10

Many thanks to all the customers who have supported us over all these years. I know at times you have been inconvenienced: when the weather has been bad, there are seafood shortages, and then when the holiday season is on, service is not always as good as we would like. But we thank you sincerely for "sticking with us".

When I look back over the years to the time after the war when my husband returned once again to civilian life and we reopened my parents' little cafe on the beach, it's hard to believe we have come so far. Whatever parents do, it's never too much if it's of benefit to them and their children.

They were happy days, and oh, how I wish we were just beginning it all again!

SEPTEMBER (SONG) 1988

A lot of years have passed since I wrote the introduction to the first edition of this book. And, as the saying goes, a lot of water has flowed under the bridge since then — fish as well, I guess. In those ten years, the book has been popular, and I have had many letters from men and women who were very pleased with the recipes, and enjoyed hearing Doyle's story. The charities that have benefited from the royalties over the years are very grateful. From me to you, a big thank you.

Watson's Bay gets more beautiful to me every hour, every minute — Sydney Harbour, and still that gentle lap of the waves on to the beach, making a tinkling sound as they draw back, washing lightly over the shell grit. It's music to my ears, just as it was when I was a child sleeping in the front room of what is now the restaurant. I can never forget such a simple, happy memory!

I found an interesting item recently in an old book about Sydney Town, together with a photograph of the Sydney Fish Markets in 1909. "Fish is about the dearest thing one can buy," a journalist wrote at the time. He went on to say that this was one of the most extraordinary features of Sydney's food supply, although the ocean was at the city's very door. "The cost of fish is an eye-opener, and for citizens of limited means a fish meal becomes a luxury." So perhaps things haven't changed as much as we sometimes think!

Something else that hasn't changed much is the recipe for succeeding in business. I came across the following advice in a turn-of-the-century newspaper I found among my late father's possessions. I hope you enjoy it as much as I did:

How to Prosper in Business

In the first place, make up your mind to accomplish whatever you undertake; decide upon some particular employment, persevere in it. All difficulties are overcome by diligence and assiduity. Be not afraid to work with your hands, and diligently too.

"A cat in gloves catches no mice."

"He who remains in the mill grinds; not he who goes and comes."

Attend to your own business; never trust to anyone else: "A pot that belongs to too many is ill stirred and worse boiled."

Be frugal: "That which will not make a pot will make a pot-lid."

"Save the pence, and the pounds will take care of themselves."

Be abstemious: "Who dainties love shall beggars prove."

11

Rise early: "The sleepy fox catches no poultry."

"Plough deep while sluggards sleep, and you will have corn to sell and to keep."

Treat every one with respect and civility: "Everything is gained and nothing lost by courtesy."

"Good manners ensure success."

Never anticipate wealth from any other source than labour — especially never place dependence upon becoming the possessor of an inheritance: "He who waits for dead men's shoes may have to go a long time barefoot."

"He who runs after a shadow hath a wearisome race."

Above all things, never despair — God is where He was; He helps those who trust in Him.

Read not books alone, but men; and chiefly careful to read thyself.

> With a gift the miser meet;
> Proud men with obeisance greet;
> Women's silly fancies soothe;
> Give wise men their due — the truth.

Hitopadesa

Who's who in the family business nowadays? Peter, our eldest son, is in charge of Doyle's on the Beach at Watson's Bay. He is very "clued up" about Australian fish and seafood, and served with the Sydney Fish Marketing Authority for many of his young years as a fishing inspector on the north coast of New South Wales. It was the love of fishing that made him choose this particular job, and an outside one at that. He was a popular kind of a fishing inspector, I should imagine, but, as the saying goes, "Nobody loves you all of the time," and I think he confiscated a few nets and undersized fish in his time. (I must admit I've done a bit of illegal-size fishing myself. It's that feel of the bream when it plays with the bait and then you finally hook it. It feels much bigger than it really is when you are pulling it in, and when you land it you think, "I'll have it for breakfast. I'll fry it whole and watch the bones." It was always very nice for breakfast, too.) His eldest son, Peter, is now managing Doyle's on the Beach. Peter Jnr is an excellent cook and has spent time in Japan and other overseas countries noting the dishes visitors to Australia will want to find here. For instance, you will now find sashimi on our menu (and in this book) — a far cry from when Jack and I, and my mother and grandparents before us, just cooked local fish and chips!

I recently came across the cash book Jack and I kept in 1948. Here are some entries for 11 April: "weekly milk, 11s 5d; baker 8s; groceries for weekend trading 15s; extra milk 4d and a lettuce etc. [the etc. probably parsley] 1s 5½d [I must have had to send one of our children for those]; fish £2; plain flour [for batter] 2s." What wonderful days — when fish nets were thrown into the water from the beach in front of our cafe and two healthy elderly fishermen slowly pulled them in, while a third man rowing a dinghy helped to keep the net full of fish together. Oh, those memories of getting started, and that bookkeeping!

John, our second son, and his wife, Barbara, have branched out on their own in Queensland and established a Doyle's on the Beach at Rainbow Bay, Coolangatta. John still personally buys the fish for his restaurant direct from the boats that call in at Tweed Heads Co-op. He is a superb and very creative cook. (Try his Stuffed Green King Prawns on page 76.) His son, John, now also works in the business.

Michael, our third son, is very involved with our Fisherman's Wharf Restaurant at Watson's Bay and is also the accountant for our entire business. His eldest son, Jim, now manages the restaurant, and like his father is an excellent cook. Jim's brother, David, is the manager of our retail and wholesale shop at the Sydney Fish Markets at Pyrmont, where we have our own fish-cleaning rooms. We have had a long association with this outlet at the markets—you'll always find a Doyle down there cleaning fish or serving. I can honestly say that our fish is the freshest and best variety obtainable—and then perfectly filleted. We certainly have a battle getting supplies at times, though, and have to make frequent interstate trips to make sure that the fish and other seafoods we want are available.

Tim, our youngest son, is managing our newest restaurant at Circular Quay, Doyle's at the Quay—another glorious spot, where you can feast outdoors while feasting your eyes on the Opera House sails, gleaming like the scales of those beautiful, big fresh snapper I wrote about earlier, and watching the water traffic—ferries, luxury cruisers, a paddle wheeler—churning up the harbour. All reflected in a blue sky by day, and at night—fairyland.

I remember when I was a child coming home to Watson's Bay in the evening with my mother from Jetty No. 1, in the old ferry *Vaucluse*, and watching one of the first neon signs in Sydney. It was a Penfolds sign showing a bottle pouring out a glass of red wine. What a lasting impression that made on me—as I write this I have a tear in my eye that those early days will never come back. (At my age, truly, it's memories that keep you going. Sometimes I wake up with a start, thinking, "I can smell the potatoes burning. Time to fry the fish.")

Our family is growing. We have twenty grandchildren—fourteen of whom work in the family business—and now ten great-grandchildren.

My husband, Jack, still goes to the Watson's Bay office every day. He can't retire from an active life, and at our stage of life it's important to keep going, even if it sometimes means pushing ourselves. I too have a busy life and keep very late nights. I still keep a daily diary, and each day we have together is very special. I am very thankful to the Good Lord—I think He has a hand in it. I like to cook and probably spend about four hours a day in my kitchen. Every day I pass the house where I was born, and I think what a place to have been born—Watson's Bay, the spot the Good Lord worked on overtime (and with no penalty rates). Some things—places, sunrise, sunset, full moons—are just as beautiful as ever. It's a matter of taking the time to stop, look and listen. And what a sight the Harbour was on 26 January 1988, our 200th birthday—congratulations, Australia.

Whenever I sign copies of my book for people, as I often do, I always say, "Hope you enjoy the recipes in this, my cookbook. It's the best I could do." I hope all my readers enjoy them.

Thank you for buying this book—someone tonight will sleep much more comfortably than last night, thanks to the Sydney City Mission.

Sincerely,
ALICE DOYLE

Appetisers

When you have a party, you want it to be a happy, successful evening with lots of friendly chatter. It may be a cocktail party or a small buffet dinner, maybe a small celebration for a birthday or at the end of the year, or just for fun. You want to be free to mingle with your guests, and join in the laughter and the buzz of conversation going on all around you as people renew old acquaintances while they enjoy the "goodies" you have provided.

Some of the best hors d'oeuvres you can provide for such a party are made with seafoods: delicious dishes you can prepare beforehand and then serve hot or cold. If it is to be a lavish buffet party, some of the recipes can be taken from different sections of the book and cut down to size; this depends on the host or hostess. I think that for these parties it is best to keep your food pieces easy to handle and that dry mixtures are preferable, so as to protect valuable furnishings, because buffets are mostly stand-up affairs and food does get spilt.

All the appetisers in this chapter can be eaten with the fingers or with cocktail forks—ideal party foods. They are delicious served with drinks before smaller dinner parties, too. You can make them instead of a sit-down first course or, if you're feeling lavish, as well!

A few fish yarns from the old-time fishermen of Watson's Bay, just to get that party started:

Mick the Fibber, the laughing cavalier and fisherman, asked Billy Love (one of the greatest snapper set-lines fishermen): "How did you go last night, Bill?"

"Not bad," said Bill. "A couple of baskets of fair-size snapper, and would you believe it, a huge big lobster about seven pound in weight."

Mick said, "Funny thing, I caught a large lobster too last week when I was set-lining. As well as a good catch of snapper, this twenty-two pound lobster was attached."

Experienced and truthful, Bill asked, "How did it eat, Mick?"

Mick the Fibber replied, "Cripes, mate, haven't reached the lobster yet, still eating the oysters off the back of it. In a coupla days we hope to get to the lobster flesh."

Headache (a loving nickname) and Brownie were sitting outside the old boatshed at Watson's Bay, talking about where the fish were biting.

Headache said, "The jewies are on thick outside the Heads, just about the spot where the Dunbar was wrecked. I caught a huge one, and in fact it had a brass lantern in it—still alight."

"Lies!" said Brownie. "I don't believe it."

"Well," said Headache, "you take twelve pound off that fourteen-pound snapper you told me you caught inside the harbour, and I'll blow out the light in the lantern!"

PREVIOUS PAGE: Watson's Bay wharf and the first pilot steamer, before the turn of the century.

HOT HORS D'OEUVRES

ANGELS ON HORSEBACK

30 oysters on the shell or bottled
pinch basil
1 tablespoon finely chopped parsley
½ teaspoon salt

pepper
paprika
10 rashers bacon, cut into thirds

Remove oysters from shells, or drain bottled ones. Place them on a dish and coat them with basil, parsley, salt, pepper and a sprinkling of paprika.

Wrap a bacon piece around each oyster, secure with a toothpick and place oysters on the griller. Grill gently for about 8 to 10 minutes (if you have an adjustable griller, keep oysters about 10 cm (4 inches) from heat) until bacon is crisp but not dried up — remember, you have an oyster wrapped up in there and only the bacon needs cooking. Turn carefully and grill the other side in the same way.

Arrange on hot dishes, and garnish attractively.

Makes 30

OYSTER PATTIES

oyster sauce (see page 6)
worcestershire sauce
anchovy sauce (optional)
30 oysters

30 pastry cases (see recipe for Creamy Fish
Tartlets, page 22, or buy ready-made
ones)

Make the sauce, add worcestershire sauce to taste and a dash of anchovy sauce if desired. Add oysters. Spoon filling into cases, each case containing one oyster. Then warm in a moderate oven for 10 minutes. Oysters are delicious luxury morsels of food, so please do not ruin them by overcooking — they only need warming.

Arrange attractively on serving dish.

Makes 30

SKEWERED PRAWNS

*500 g (1 lb) large green prawns, peeled,
    deveined*

2 large capsicums (green peppers)

8 rashers bacon, cut into sixths

3 115 g (4 oz) cans champignons, drained

1 cup vegetable oil

1 teaspoon salt

pepper

Cut prawns into quarters.

Wash green peppers and cut into 3 cm (1 in) squares. Alternate prawn, bacon, mushrooms and green pepper on 48 small skewers or round toothpicks, the toothpicks about 8 cm (3 in) long.

Place kebabs on a well-greased griller. Combine oil, salt and pepper to taste and brush kebabs with sauce.

Grill quickly, brushing with oil mixture and turning until cooked (10 to 15 minutes).

NOTE: You can make these earlier on the day of the party, but please be careful when reheating them. Remember, preheat oven to very hot, then lower temperature when you put the seafood in. Seafoods cook in a few minutes, and the prawns will be ruined if cooked too long.

Makes about 48

LOBSTER BITES

250 g (8 oz) cooked lobster meat, fresh or frozen

*24 fresh mushrooms, about 4 cm (1½ in)
    in diameter*

¼ cup condensed cream of mushroom soup

2 tablespoons fine, soft breadcrumbs

2 tablespoons mayonnaise or salad dressing

¼ teaspoon worcestershire sauce

few drops tabasco sauce

pepper

grated parmesan cheese

If your lobster is frozen, let it thaw naturally (don't stand it in warm water or run water on to it), and make sure that all particles of shell have been removed. Chop the lobster meat.

Rinse mushrooms in cold water, dry them and remove stems. Combine soup, lobster, breadcrumbs, mayonnaise, worcestershire sauce, tabasco sauce and pepper to taste. Mix together well. Fill each mushroom cap with a tablespoon of the lobster mixture, sprinkle with cheese and place on a well-greased baking sheet.

Bake in a hot oven (220°C, 425°F) for 10 to 15 minutes, or until lightly browned. Decorate with your usual flair.

Makes 24

SASHIMI—A GOURMET'S DELIGHT *(PAGE 29)*

MICKY DRIP'S SEAFOOD CHOWDER *(PAGE 49)*

FISH COCKTAIL PIECES

3 cups plain flour
salt and pepper
dash tabasco sauce
4 cups (or more) water
oil or beef dripping for deep-frying

1.5 kg (3 lb) fillets of any thick type of fish,
such as gemfish, jewfish or kingfish
parsley
lemon wedges
tartare sauce (see page 56)

To make batter, place flour, salt, pepper and tabasco sauce into a fairly large basin. Add water. With your hand-held egg beater, beat water into flour until the mixture is thick and creamy. If mixture is too thick, gradually add more water to make it similar to the consistency of pancake batter — plenty of beating does the trick. This is a simple batter, but I find it is the best.

Place oil, deep enough to practically cover the fish pieces, into a large, deep pan. (Please note that the oil or dripping must not have been used before if you want this recipe to be a success.) Heat oil till practically boiling. (I have never seen that blue flame they say appears when it is time to start frying — do your own test by dropping a little batter in the hot oil, and when it rises fast to the top, you will know it is ready.)

Have your fish pieces ready, cut to the size you require — I always make them a little larger than most people do, otherwise they seem to be all batter. Lightly dust each portion with flour, then dip in batter and drop carefully into the hot oil.

Cook for about 10 minutes. Do not overcook — fish is delicate and cooks very quickly — and remember that unless you serve the fish cocktails immediately you will have to reheat them.

When cooked, drain well. Please do not put one on top of another after all your hard work; they will become soggy if you do.

If you need to reheat the fish, make sure the oven is very hot (260°C, 500°F), then lower the temperature to about 150°C (300°F) when fish pieces are put in. Please do not dry up these tasty mosels of fish — 10 minutes in the oven is plenty.

Spread sheets of greaseproof paper on your serving dishes and arrange fish pieces on these. Garnish with parsley galore, lemon wedges and small bowls of tartare sauce.

Ah, that eye appeal. You can get away with the greatest flop as long as it looks good — funny, isn't it?

Makes 20

SAVOURY SCONES

A bite of one of these piquant scones and then some Fish Cocktail Pieces — very tasty. Don't worry, you will quickly learn the art of scone making. The first scones I made, my husband nailed to a wall — so never give up.

3 cups self-raising flour

1 onion, grated

salt

2 tablespoons butter

1 egg

2 cups milk (must be room temperature or lukewarm)

1½ extra tablespoons butter

1 teaspoon French mustard

¼ teaspoon cayenne pepper

1 cup grated strong cheese (preferably parmesan)

parsley

First, preheat oven at highest temperature.

In your mixing bowl put flour, onion and ¼ teaspoon salt. Rub butter into flour mixture until it resembles fine breadcrumbs.

Beat egg and milk together and add quickly to the mixture. It should be fairly moist — if too moist, use more flour; if too dry, use more milk. Turn mixture out on to a floured board and knead. Keep your hands well floured and handle the mixture quickly; but make sure you knead it until it's nice and smooth, with no roughness on top.

Use your floured rolling pin to roll the dough out to about 1 cm (½ in) thick. Cut out small rounds and place them on a greased baking sheet. Put aside while the cheese topping is prepared.

To make topping, put extra butter, mustard, cayenne pepper, cheese and a pinch of salt into a saucepan. Cook for about 5 minutes until well blended.

Spread topping on scone rounds and bake in a very hot oven on the highest shelf for about 15 minutes, or until cooked.

Turn scones out on to a clean teatowel and wrap loosely till needed.

These savoury scones taste delicious with fish savouries and all your other cocktail pieces. Please make them look attractive with parsley. Of course, serve hot if possible.

Makes about 24

FISH CROQUETTES

1.5 kg (3 lb) fish (try gemfish, jewfish,
  kingfish or mullet), with skin and
  bones removed. (Smile nicely at your
  fishmonger and he may remove the
  skin for you.)

freshly ground pepper

2 large stalks celery, chopped

1 large onion, chopped

1 bay leaf, finely crushed

3 drops tabasco sauce

good pinch basil

water

1 kg (2lb) potatoes, boiled and mashed

1 dessertspoon anchovy paste or sauce

2 tablespoons chopped parsley

1 egg

½ cup milk

¾ cup plain flour

extra plain flour

oil for deep-frying

parsley

lemon wedges

tartare sauce (see page 56)

Chop fish finely and place in a large saucepan. Add a little pepper to taste, celery, onion, bay leaf, tabasco and basil. Add water to come about 5 cm (2 in) above fish and cook slowly, covered, for 20 minutes.

Pour boiled mixture into mixing bowl. Add mashed potatoes, anchovy paste or sauce, chopped parsley, the egg beaten into the milk, ¾ cup plain flour and ground pepper. Mix together until you have a moist mixture you can handle, and shape into small cakes.

Spread the extra flour on your chopping board and coat the fish cakes. Fry in oil, as for Fish Cocktail Pieces (see page 19) and follow the same instructions.

These are delicious, but care must be taken not to overcook—especially if they are to be warmed up.

Serves 6

CRUNCHY CELERY FISHWICH

2 sticks crisp celery, strings removed and finely
  chopped

1 tablespoon mayonnaise

sprinkle paprika

pinch basil

2 cups cooked, boned, flaked fish

salt and pepper

small french loaf, sliced horizontally and
  buttered

Combine celery, mayonnaise, paprika, basil, fish and salt and pepper in blender or beat together in a basin till well mixed. Spread mixture on bread halves and join together. Can be warmed in oven before serving.

21

CREAMY FISH TARTLETS

This is a really delicious mixture and can be used for so many dishes. You can buy ready-made patty cases; or you can make your own.

Pastry

1 cup self-raising flour

1 cup plain flour

170 g (6 oz) margarine, lard or clarified fat

1/8 teaspoon salt

1 egg

1 cup water

Filling

1 kg (2 lb) flaked and boned fish (gemfish, jewfish, snapper, whitebait,* canned salmon,* or whatever you have on hand)

salt and freshly ground pepper

1 teaspoon anchovy essence or paste

2 large sticks celery, finely chopped

1 large carrot, finely grated

1 tablespoon chopped parsley

pinch basil

1 tablespoon chives

1 bay leaf, crushed

1 onion, finely chopped (optional)

dash tabasco sauce

½ cup milk

½ cup water

2 tablespoons plain flour, blended with a little milk

paprika

parsley

To make pastry, sift self-raising flour, plain flour and salt together. Rub shortening into flour till it resembles fine breadcrumbs. Beat egg and water together, add to flour and mix well.

Turn out on to a floured board and, using your floured rolling pin (or a milk bottle, if you cannot find the pin), roll out thinly. If the dough is too hard to roll, put back into bowl, add a little more water and try again. Cut out rounds and press lightly into patty tins.

To make filling, mix together fish, salt, pepper, anchovy essence or paste, celery, carrot, chopped parsley, basil, chives, bay leaf, tabasco sauce and onion, if liked. Put all into a saucepan with milk and water to almost cover the mixture—enough to make it fairly moist. Boil slowly for about 10 minutes and thicken with blended flour. Cook for a further 10 minutes, stirring constantly—please be careful that it does not burn.

Allow the mixture to cool a little. Then fill the pastry-lined patty tins and bake in a hot oven for about 20 minutes. Turn the tartlets out, arrange on a serving dish and garnish each one with a sprinkling of paprika and parsley sprigs.

Serve amongst your other hot savouries, or make a feature dish of them.

*NOTE: If using whitebait or canned salmon, make your sauce first, then add fish and cook for 5 minutes only. Also, if you do not want to make pastry, make your cases with sandwich bread. Butter patty tins and one side of bread. Carefully place bread, buttered side down, in tins. Trim and bake. You can then put the filling in when they are cooked—and, of course, you will reheat when ready.

Makes 18

ROE TIT BITS

4 large fresh soft fish roes (flathead roes are good)
8 thin strips bacon
lemon juice
salt
butter for frying

8 pieces of fried bread or buttered toast
  (preferably rye) with crusts removed
anchovy paste
pickled gherkin, cut in strips
freshly ground pepper

Cut the roes in half lengthwise. Fold each half in two, wrap a strip of bacon around them. Sprinkle with lemon juice and salt and secure with small skewers, string or toothpicks.

Fry gently in hot butter or bake in a hot oven till crisp. In the meantime, spread the fried bread or toast with anchovy paste and add a few strips of gherkin, cover with buttered greaseproof paper and heat in the oven.

When roes are cooked, remove the skewers, sprinkle with freshly ground pepper, place roes on toast or fried bread and serve very hot.

Serves 5–6

CRUMBED ROES

Flathead roes are tender, smooth and flavoursome. I like to prepare them very simply.

flathead or mullet roes
1 egg
breadcrumbs

butter
lemon wedges

Place roes in a saucepan of warm water, bring to boil and simmer 5 minutes for flathead roes, 15 minutes for mullet roes. Drain. Cool, brush with beaten egg, roll in breadcrumbs and fry in butter until nicely browned.

Serve warm with lemon wedges and toast.

Allow 1 flathead roe or ½ large mullet roe per person.

SALMON IN A WRAP

Country readers far from the sea who must rely on canned seafood need not despair. Many city dwellers have no access to fresh fish either, and there are many delicious hot hors d'oeuvres to be made with canned seafood. This recipe, and those following, are good ones to try.

Pastry

250 g (8 oz) butter or margarine

1 egg

1 cup water

pinch salt

1 cup self-raising flour

1½ cups plain flour

Filling

250 g (8 oz) can red salmon

¼ cup mayonnaise or salad dressing

1 tablespoon lemon juice

1 teaspoon horseradish

1 teaspoon grated onion

paprika

Beat butter until it creams (always have your butter soft to the point of oiliness, as it is much easier to beat), add egg beaten with the cup of water, slowly add the sifted flours to which salt has been added. The pastry must be easy to handle, so you may need to add a little more water. If moist enough, turn on to a floured board, divide into two pieces and roll as thinly as possible into circles 23 cm (9 in) in diameter.

To make filling, drain and flake salmon. Add mayonnaise, lemon juice, horseradish and onion, mixing all together thoroughly. Spread each pastry circle with ½ cup salmon mixture and cut each round into 16 wedge-shaped pieces. Roll up, beginning at the round edge and rolling towards the point. Place rolls on a baking tray and prick to allow steam to escape. Sprinkle with paprika. Bake in a hot oven, about 220°C (425°F), for about 15 or 20 minutes until lightly browned.

If you would like more filling, use a larger quantity of salmon, or salmon and tuna mixed. If you substitute tuna for salmon, be sure to keep the mixture moist.

The rolls can be made beforehand and reheated. Make sure the oven is hot before putting the cooked rolls in, then decrease heat to the lowest point so as not to dry out the salmon. With this dish I use the cocktail sauce on page 57. Serve on hot plates with lots of garnishes.

Makes about 32

DANCER'S DELIGHT

This recipe was given to me by Joy Lodge, in her early days a dancer of distinction and for many years a well-known figure at St Luke's Hospital, Sydney, where she worked in the office and at the reception desk. The dish may be prepared beforehand and popped in the oven just before serving.

1 can sardines or 6 king prawns, shelled

juice of 1 lemon or a little water or vinegar

3 gherkins

onion

salt

parsley, finely chopped

finely chopped celery

pepper (cayenne if preferred)

6 pastry boats

small quantity mashed potato

Mash sardines with lemon, water or vinegar (if using prawns, squeeze juice over them). Add 2 of the gherkins, chopped (keep one for garnishing), onion, salt, parsley, celery and pepper. Place mixture in pastry boats.

Cover with mashed potato, streaked with a fork or left plain. Garnish with thin rounds of remaining gherkin and place on a tray or pavlova plate. Put in a moderate oven or under the griller for slow heating and browning. Garnish with more parsley.

Serves 6

TUNA CHEESIES

30 rounds Melba toast

250 g (8 oz) can tuna, drained

1 cup shredded cheese

¼ cup butter or margarine, softened

2 tablespoons lemon juice

1½ tablespoons grated onion

1 teaspoon worcestershire sauce

½ teaspoon paprika

3 drops tabasco

Make Melba toast first — this is simply thinly sliced bread baked in a hot oven till crisp.

Flake tuna; cream the cheese and butter. Add seasonings and tuna. Mix thoroughly. Spread each Melba toast round with approximately 2 teaspoonsful of tuna mixture.

Place on a baking tray, and grill about 10 cm (4 in) from source of heat for 3 to 5 minutes or until browned.

Makes about 30

CRAB GRABS

250 g (8 oz) can crab meat

1 packet Golden Puff biscuits
 (or pastry rounds, biscuit thin)

½ cup shredded cheese

2 tablespoons mayonnaise or salad dressing

1½ teaspoons chopped chives

2 drops tabasco

freshly ground pepper

¼ teaspoon salt

2 egg whites

Chop crab meat and put aside. Split biscuits in half, and place in a warm oven on a greased baking slide for about 10 minutes. (Pastry rounds will take a little longer. Cook until light brown, remove from oven and turn over.)

Blend cheese, mayonnaise, chives, tabasco, pepper and crab meat. Mix thoroughly.

Add salt to egg whites, beat until stiff but not dry. Fold crab mixture into egg white. Top each biscuit with 1 tablespoon of crab mixture. Bake in a very hot oven, 230°C (450°F), for 8 to 10 minutes or until lightly browned.

Makes 20

TUNA PUFFS

Puff Shells

½ cup boiling water

¼ cup butter or margarine

pinch salt

½ cup plain flour

2 eggs

Tuna Filling

500 g (16 oz) tuna

1 cup celery, strings removed and finely chopped

½ cup mayonnaise or salad dressing

2 tablespoons chopped onion

2 tablespoons sweet pickles, chopped

salt to taste

Combine water, butter and salt in a saucepan and bring to boil. Add flour all at once and stir vigorously until mixture forms a ball and leaves the sides of the pan.

Remove from heat. Cool for a while, then add eggs, one at a time, beating thoroughly after each addition. Continue beating until a stiff dough is formed. (If you are making puffs for the first time — and there always has to be a first time — use your saucepan to do all this, especially if you are making only a small amount. You will become such an addict of puff making that you will be making chocolate eclairs and cream puffs in no time.)

When the mixture is smooth and thick, drop level teaspoonfuls on to a well-greased baking sheet, and bake in a very hot oven, 230°C (450°F), for 10 minutes. Reduce heat to 175°C (350°F) and continue baking about 5 to 10 minutes longer. Cool.

To make filling, drain and flake tuna. Combine all ingredients and mix thoroughly. Cut tops from puff shells and fill each shell with about 2 teaspoons of mixture. These are served cold (but they are included with the hot hors d'oeuvres because they are cooked).

Makes about 40

COLD HORS D'OEUVRES

PRAWNS

To me, prawns always look best unpeeled; that beautiful, red, shining shell is most attractive. (You can always rub them with oil to make them look even better if you have the time.) But, alas, you are not having a prawn night, so you will have to peel them, I'm afraid. If you are like me and just love prawns, get somebody else who is allergic to eating them to do the peeling. Otherwise, the temptation may be so overpowering that you will have to cross prawns off the menu! Shell the prawns, leaving the tails on to hold them by. Make sure the prawns are deveined and cleaned properly. Arrange them on platters around bowls containing dips (see page 57), close together and all facing the one way, with parsley galore. Have finger bowls and serviettes nearby.

Another way with whole prawns is to spread a cracker biscuit with mayonnaise, top with a prawn, then glaze with gelatine (see recipe for glaze on page 124).

You will find other prawn recipes on pages 73-83.

OUR GREAT AUSTRALIAN ROCK OYSTER

If you want to be lavish at your cocktail party, place oysters on plates with small containers of cocktail sauce in the centre. Opened oysters dry out very quickly, so they are a very "dicey" item for a cocktail party. Don't leave them uncovered, either in or out of the fridge. Cover them with damp greaseproof paper if they have to stand any length of time, and keep cool in the refrigerator. I suggest you serve lots of thinly sliced brown or rye bread with your oysters — they'll go further that way. I hope you know, too, that oysters can vary in size and taste, depending on the season.

You can obtain small disposable forks for the oysters — they are plastic, very reasonably priced and a great saving with the washing up. Anyway, it's so easy to scrape little oyster forks into the rubbish bin, with the shells, that it's a very good idea to use the plastic ones.

Finely cracked ice is good as a bed for oysters, but a nuisance at parties.

If you would like to serve oysters cooked, the following recipes are popular ones. There are other oyster recipes in the Seafoods section (see pages 99-105).

SEAFOOD EGGS

500 g (1 lb) cooked lobster meat (fresh or
  frozen), chopped very finely, or 500 g (1 lb)
  peeled prawns, fresh or frozen, chopped
¾ cup mayonnaise or salad dressing
½ teaspoon chilli sauce
1 teaspoon finely chopped capsicum

1 teaspoon grated onion
pinch salt
1 tablespoon chopped parsley
16 hard-boiled eggs
thinly sliced red capsicum

Defrost lobster or prawns if frozen.

Combine lobster meat, mayonnaise, chilli sauce, capsicum, onion, tabasco sauce and salt.

Cut eggs in half lengthwise and remove yolks. Fill each egg white with 1 tablespoon of the lobster mixture. Sprinkle with chopped parsley and chill.

Just before serving, place a strip of red capsicum across each egg—remember, eye appeal does the trick every time.

NOTE: Don't discard those unused egg yolks—they'll make a beautiful dressing for your other dishes (see Leghorn Sauce, page 59).

Makes 32

SASHIMI

The most important thing with this recipe is to use very fresh, good-quality
ingredients.

150 g (5 oz) very fresh tuna
150 g (5 oz) very fresh kingfish
150 g (5 oz) very fresh ocean trout
150 g (5 oz) grated white radish

wasabi paste or powder (available from
  Japanese food shops)
soy sauce

Cut tuna into a rectangular block about 5 cm by 20 cm (2 in by 8 in) and 2 cm (¾ in) thick. Then slice sideways into 1 cm (½ in) wide strips. Cut kingfish and ocean trout in the same way.

Arrange fish slices artistically on a serving plate. Add grated white radish, and place a small amount of wasabi on side of plate. (If using wasabi powder, mix with a little water.) Serve soy sauce in individual small bowls.

Mix a small amount of wasabi with some soy sauce and dip fish into this before eating.

Serves 4

COME HITHER STARTERS

My thanks to Dr Lola Power, formerly of St Luke's Hospital, Sydney, for giving me one of her delicious recipes.

6 lemons (1 per person)

2 large cans best-quality sardines, in olive oil

2 hard-boiled eggs, chopped finely

some anchovy paste to flavour

salt and freshly ground pepper

1 tablespoon vodka

1 tablespoon chopped parsley

2 teaspoons chopped chives

2–3 tablespoons thick mayonnaise

paprika

6 stuffed olives

Procure fresh, shining, good-quality lemons. Cut in two, scoop out pulp and retain it for later use. Mix all remaining ingredients together, except paprika and olives, to make a smooth paste.

Fill cavity of lemon shell with the mixture and sprinkle paprika on top sparingly. Top with ½ stuffed olive. Place on decorated savoury plate with spoons.

This can be served with pre-dinner drinks or as an entree.

Serves 6

GEORGE HEYDON'S COLD FISH PUFFS

Thanks to my old friend and one-time hotel chef George Heydon for this recipe.

1 kg (2 lb) boned fish fillets, steamed
salt and pepper
750 g (1½ lb) potatoes, boiled and mashed
2 tablespoons plain flour

1 egg
oil for frying
lemon wedges
tartare sauce

Flake the fish and season with salt and pepper to taste. Put aside.

Put the mashed potato in a bowl, add the flour and as much egg as necessary to make a smooth dough.

Place the potato mixture onto a floured board, pat out (with floured hands) to a thickness of about 15 mm (½ in). Cut into 8 cm (3 in) rounds, spoon a little of the fish on each round and gently pat down. Fold over and press the edges together.

Heat the oil in a pan and gently fry the puffs on both sides until golden brown.

Drain, allow to cool, and then chill in the refrigerator. Serve with lemon wedges and tartare sauce (page 56), if you like.

Makes about 25–30

CREAMS OF THE SEA

thinly sliced bread
cream cheese or cheese spread
Gemfish Spread (see page 33) or smoked salmon,
  salmon, caviar, sardines, pickled herring,
  chopped lobster, crab or prawns

red and green pepper, finely chopped
stuffed olives
parsley, finely chopped

Cut fancy shapes (stars, diamonds, circles, etc.) from thinly sliced white, wholewheat or rye bread. Spread with cream cheese or cheese spread and top with rolled smoked salmon, Gemfish Spread or any of the other suggested toppings. Garnish with additional cream cheese forced through a pastry tube and a little chopped pepper, stuffed olives or parsley. A little trouble, but worth it for a delicious hors d'oeuvre.

SMOKED ROES

smoked mullet roes
bread rusks

lemon juice
olives, plain or stuffed

Mullet roes are delicious smoked, but because this is so much trouble to do yourself, it is better to buy them ready smoked. Cut the roes into pieces and serve on round or square rusks (available from delicatessens.) Add a squeeze of lemon juice and serve with a variety of olives.

CUCUMBER AND FINELY FLAKED FISH SANDWICHES

cucumber, finely sliced
cold cooked flaked fish
white onion, grated
lettuce leaves

salt and pepper
rye bread, buttered
parsley

Sprinkle the sliced cucumber with salt, leave to drain, pat dry and season with a little pepper.

Mix fish and onion.

Place cucumber slices on buttered rye bread, cover with fish mixture, and top with lettuce before closing sandwich. Trim sandwich, and shape to please.

Garnish with parsley.

Spreads, Dips & Pâté

Gemfish Spread

gemfish, skinned, boned and chopped

water

salt

sliced onion

celery, finely chopped

few drops tabasco

bay leaf

freshly ground pepper

butter

cream

anchovy sauce (optional)

parsley

Put whatever quantity of gemfish you think you may need in water to cover with salt, onion, celery, tabasco, bay leaf and pepper. Bring to the boil, cook for 10 minutes.

When cooked, strain and mash and add enough butter and cream to make into a smooth spread. A teaspoon of anchovy sauce or anchovette adds extra flavour.

Spread on bread shapes or biscuits and decorate with finely chopped parsley.

Curried Fish Spread

2 tablespoons white sauce (see page 61)

1 cup cold cooked fish (gemfish is ideal), boned and skinned

1 cup cold cooked smoked haddock or cod

salt and pepper

1 teaspoon curry powder

parsley

Make the white sauce and put aside. Pound the fish in a mortar, or blend to a fine paste in an electric blender.

Season with a little salt and pepper, then add the paste and curry powder to the white sauce. Place in a saucepan and heat very gently for a few minutes, stirring all the time. Do not allow mixture to boil. Remove from heat and cool.

When cold, spread on bread and butter or biscuits, and garnish with parsley.

PRAWN AND BRANDY SAVOURY SPREAD

If you don't like this recipe when you try it, never mind—next time you have prawns, eat them plain and drink the brandy!

500 g (1 lb) cooked or green prawns
½ cup dry white wine
90 g (3 oz) butter
4 drops tabasco
salt and freshly ground pepper
1 stick celery, finely chopped
pinch nutmeg
pinch cayenne pepper

juice of 1 lemon
½ cup fish stock (from green prawns, if used)
  or water
1 tablespoon brandy
sprinkle paprika
melted butter for sealing
lemon juice

If using green prawns, cover them with water, add salt, bring to the boil and simmer 8 minutes. Drain prawns, reserving stock.

Peel prawns, put in blender with wine, butter, tabasco, salt and pepper, celery, nutmeg, cayenne, lemon juice and stock and blend for one minute or until smooth. Remove from blender, add brandy and paprika. Pack in small jars, seal with melted butter and screw lids on tightly. The spread should keep for 3 to 4 days in the refrigerator.

Serve on fingers of hot buttered toast or on savoury biscuits and sprinkle with lemon juice. If you don't have a blender, this can be made in the old-fashioned way with a mortar and pestle.

TANTALISING SARDINE DIP OR SPREAD

2 125 g (4 oz) cans sardines
500 g (16 oz) cream cheese, softened
1 tablespoon horseradish
2 drops tabasco

3 tablespoons lemon juice
2 tablespoons grated onion
½ cup crushed potato crisps
2 tablespoons chopped parsley

Drain sardines and mash. Cream the cheese, add horseradish, tabasco, lemon juice, onion and sardines and mix thoroughly. Shape into a mound on a serving plate. Combine potato crisps and parsley and cover sardine mixture completely. Chill.

Serve with breads, crackers or mixed raw vegetables.

Makes about 3 cups

FISHERMAN'S WHARF GARLIC PRAWNS *(PAGE 79)*

MUSSELS A LA PORTUGUESE *(PAGE 106)*

TARAMASALATA 1

This delicious first course is courtesy of George Andronicus. It is a favourite
Greek dish.

1 can tarama (fish roe) (100 g or 3½ oz)
1 egg yolk
4 slices stale white bread
1 clove garlic, crushed
½ small onion, finely grated

3-4 tablespoons lemon juice
½ cup olive oil
bread or raw vegetables, cut in strips

Put tarama and egg yolk in blender, mix at low speed and add bread (which has been soaked in water and squeezed out), garlic and onion and blend. When well blended, add lemon juice and olive oil. Chill.

Serve on a platter with crusty bread or crisp vegetables such as celery, carrot, cauliflower, zucchini.

TARAMASALATA 2

This taramasalata recipe was given to me by Marika Harris, a Greek lady
with a grown-up family — and in my opinion a great cook.

1 can tarama (100 g or 3½ oz)
  or other salted fish roe
2 medium potatoes, boiled
1 cup olive oil
juice of 2 lemons

1 onion
chives, finely chopped
crackers
black olives

Using a mortar and pestle, pound fish roe and potatoes to make a fine paste. Still using the pestle, add alternate small amounts of oil and lemon juice until all is used. The mixture should be creamy, smooth and thick.

When ready to use, add grated onion and chives. Spread on cracker biscuits and decorate with halved black olives for delicious canapes.

35

Do Drop In Salmon Spread

2 large brown onions, finely sliced	*2 tablespoons lemon juice*
butter	*1 teaspoon worcestershire sauce*
1 teaspoon sugar	*pinch basil*
1 large can red salmon	*few drops tabasco*
1 cup sour cream	*¼ teaspoon salt*

Fry sliced onions gently in a little butter until soft, mix in sugar.

Drain salmon, reserving liquid in case needed. Mash salmon, add onions and all other ingredients together. Make the spread very moist—if it seems too dry, add some of the juice from the salmon.

Serve with potato crisps or savoury biscuits.

Makes about 2½ cups

Redfish Paste with Bacon

500 g (1 lb) redfish fillets, skinned and boned	*freshly ground pepper*
1 rasher bacon, rind removed, finely chopped	*paprika*
90 g (3 oz) butter	*2 drops tabasco*
juice of 1 lemon	*2 teaspoons brandy*
1 egg	*melted butter for sealing*

Put redfish and bacon through a food processor, using the plastic blade, or else mince together very finely in an ordinary mincing machine.

Put in saucepan with butter, and using a wooden spoon, stir continually over low heat until cooked, about 6 minutes.

Add lemon juice and stir in well, then add beaten egg.

Allow to cool and add freshly ground pepper, paprika, tabasco and brandy. Pack in clean sterilised jars, sealing with melted butter before screwing lids on tightly. This should keep for 3 to 4 days in the refrigerator.

Serve on hot buttered toast or savoury biscuits.

SUMMER FISH PÂTÉ

I think this is a truly delicious fish pâté, and my gourmet friends agree. The true flavour of fish comes through in a delicate smooth pâté which you do not have to be a professional to make. In a food processor it's a breeze, in a blender the same—but a word of warning here: don't overdo the blending. The pâté can also be made in the old-fashioned way with a mortar and pestle, and even in a bowl with a wooden spoon, although this takes more time.

1 kg (2 lb) raw fish, boned and skinned	pinch nutmeg
1 onion	½ teaspoon salad herbs
salt and pepper	4 drops tabasco
bouquet garni (rosemary, basil, 2 bay leaves, dill)	2 teaspoons gelatine
	½ cup fish stock
1 large stick celery	juice and finely grated rind of 1 lemon
125 g (4 oz) butter	2 hard-boiled eggs, sliced
1 carrot, grated	chopped parsley
2 tablespoons cream	paprika

Place fish, onion, salt, pepper, herbs and celery in a saucepan, cover with water, bring to boil and simmer 15 minutes. When cool, strain through a fine strainer. Keep the stock and flake the cooked fish.

Place butter in blender (softened butter if you use a food processor) and add carrot, cream, nutmeg, salad herbs, tabasco, freshly ground pepper and a pinch of salt. Blend for a few seconds, gradually add all but ½ cup of stock, then cooked fish, blend for a few seconds until smooth. Taste the mixture and correct flavouring, then turn into a flat pyrex dish or round glass tart plate. Smooth the surface.

Make a gelatine glaze by dissolving gelatine in ½ cup of hot fish stock, add lemon juice and rind. Pour over pâté. Place egg slices in a pattern around top of pâté, and press gently into glaze. Sprinkle with chopped parsley, a little paprika and a little freshly ground pepper.

If you don't want to go to the trouble of glazing your pâté, simple decorate with chopped parsley and paprika for colour.

Serves 6–8

Soups & Chowders

Do you know just how many delicious and nourishing meals can be made out of the backbones and the heads of fish? Well, the imaginative cook can make the most wonderful dishes, and once she becomes acquainted with her fish supplier, he can become one of her best friends in the culinary field. What better or more nourishing food for the family — especially when served with the flair of the professional with vegetables grated finely, toasted sippets, Melba toast, cheese and luscious cream.

But please don't say to your guests or to your family: "Have some fish soup." Give it a fancy name: "We are having seafood bisque tonight." And don't forget to have lashings of hot fried bread or garlic bread, and salt and freshly ground pepper, on the table.

TOHEROA SOUP

I am indebted to Elsa Jacoby, MBE, for this delicious Toheroa Soup. Elsa Jacoby is a much-loved and well-known personality in Sydney, and an untiring worker for charity.

1 can toheroas or clams, drained
3 cups fish stock (see opposite)
salt and pepper to taste

whipped cream
nutmeg

Puree the toheroas or clams in a blender, place in pot with fish stock, season to taste. Stir well while heating and simmer gently about 30 to 40 minutes.

Serve in hot dishes garnished with cream and nutmeg.

NOTE: Clams are the tasty Australian alternative to toheroas but, of course, lack the lovely green colour.

Serves 3–4

PREVIOUS PAGE: My parents' Signal Dining Rooms at Signal Hill, 1900.

FISH STOCK

There will be times when you are cooking and you will have the small fish you or the kids have caught, or you have filleted a big snapper that was won in one of those pub raffles. Or, if you're lucky, the prawn glut is on and you are flat out peeling to make some curried prawns or garlic prawns. With these little fish, snapper bones or heads, or the prawn shells, you are going to make stock for some of your seafood dishes. This will be a strong-flavoured stock with body, and here is a simple way to make it.

3 fish skeletons, including well-scaled heads   *1 teaspoon salt*
water

Wash fish pieces thoroughly and put in a heavy saucepan or stewpan. Add salt and fill the pan with water. Bring to a boil, then simmer (but still on the boil) for 1 hour. If the bones and heads are large and you have a fair amount, cook longer.

If you want to keep some of the flesh from the heads and bones, take them out and put the flesh aside after they have been cooking for ½ hour. Put the remains back in the pot and continue cooking.

Strain stock very carefully through a fine strainer or sieve, and make sure you do not let one bone, particle of shell, or scale through.

When cold, refrigerate the stock until needed. After a day, the stock will be a jelly. You now have the basic foundation for any soup or seafood dishes you want to create.

If you make stock a couple of days before you are going to use it, omit salt. In any case, keep stock no longer than 2 days (unless, of course, you freeze it).

Makes enough for 8 people

MOCK TOHEROA SOUP

A bit of trivia told to me at random by George Heydon.

3 cups Cream of Snapper Soup (see opposite)
195 g (6½ oz) tin cooked mussels, drained
2 teaspoons swede turnip, grated

little spinach juice for colour
½ cup cream
lemon juice to taste

With the snapper soup as the base, add mussels, swede turnip, and the spinach juice, which makes the greenish tinge of real toheroa. Heat well.

Add cream and squeeze lemon juice into the mixture.

Serves 5

CREAM OF SNAPPER SOUP

John Doyle's speciality!
Get those taste buds working for this one. Ask yourself: "Is there something missing?" Add more anchovy essence or seasoning if you like, but go easy to keep that fish flavour.

8 cups fish stock (see page 41)

2 large potatoes, whole, peeled

2 large brown onions, chopped finely

4 stalks celery, chopped finely

½ cup rice or sago

1 teaspoon basil

4 drops tabasco sauce

1 or 2 bay leaves, to taste

1 teaspoon salt

pepper

½ cup plain flour

1 cup milk (more may be needed)

2 teaspoons curry (optional)

2 teaspoons anchovy sauce

2 or 3 large carrots, grated

chopped parsley

Heat the fish stock, add the potatoes, onions, celery, rice, basil, tabasco, bay leaves, salt and pepper. Cook for ½ hour, then thicken with plain flour mixed to a smooth paste with the cup of milk. Add the curry powder if you're using it.

Let the flour cook through the mixture until you cannot taste it. Add anchovy sauce, stir in well, and a few minutes before the soup is ready, put in the grated carrot. Garnish with parsley.

Serve this soup boiling hot with sippets of fried bread or dry toast.

NOTE: This is an excellent soup for special diets and invalids. By omitting the flour, you can put in more vegetables. Just before serving you can add the fish you picked from the bones and heads when you were making your fish stock, if you like.

Serves 8

OYSTER SOUP

Top marks for this soup. It's a very old recipe and full of the good things needed for a delicious, nourishing soup. It's work, but worth the effort for all the praise you receive.

fish bones for stock

3 cups milk

2 cups fish stock (see page 41) or water

1 carrot, sliced

1 small brown onion, chopped

2 bay leaves

pinch basil

4 peppercorns

salt

60 g (2 oz) butter

1 tablespoon flour

2 egg yolks, beaten

1 cup cream

2 dozen oysters on the shell or bottled

few drops tabasco sauce

1 teaspooon worcestershire sauce

finely chopped parsley

Cut fish bones into small pieces; put them in a saucepan with milk, water, carrot, onion, bay leaves, basil, peppercorns and salt. Simmer gently for ½ hour. Strain. Discard bones, vegetables and seasonings.

Melt the butter in a pan, stir in the flour, add the strained fish stock, stir until boiling and cook for 3 to 5 minutes.

Beat the egg yolks and cream together, strain into the soup and stir for a few minutes, taking care that the soup does not boil. Carefully place oysters in, add tabasco sauce and worcestershire sauce. Serve immediately, so that the oysters are just warmed through.

Garnish with parsley and serve with fried croutons, if you like.

NOTE: If you use bottled oysters, discard water they are in and rinse before using.

Serves 4

BOUILLABAISSE 1

6 small fillets fish (cod, gemfish or other white
   fish), fried
3 tablespoons vegetable oil
1 Spanish or brown onion, sliced finely
60 g (2 oz) rice flour or cornflour
6 cups fish stock (see page 41)

2 egg yolks
½ cup white wine
2 tablespoons cream
salt and pepper to taste
chopped parsley
paprika

Fry the fish in vegetable oil. Set aside. Fry onion until golden brown in the same oil. Stir in rice flour or cornflour; add the stock and stir until it boils. Remove the scum as it rises, then cover and simmer gently for ½ hour.

Take off stove and run through a fine sieve. Beat the egg yolks and add the cream to them. Return the saucepan to the stove and bring nearly to boiling point. Strain the yolk mixture into the soup and stir on a low flame until the soup thickens slightly. Make sure it doesn't boil, or it may curdle. Add the wine, salt and pepper. Place the fish fillets in a tureen and pour the soup over them. Sprinkle with parsley and paprika. Serve with fried croutons and lemon.

Serves 5–6

BOUILLABAISSE 2

Alice Doyle tells all: how to make really great bouillabaisse. My grandfather, Henry Newton, a fisherman of Watson's Bay, called this "fish soup". He had a hut on the foreshores of Coolong Road in Vaucluse and kept his boats there, mended nets, and took many of the well-known gentlemen of Sydney fishing. With the catch he would make this fish soup. Fattening? You bet it is! Delicious? You bet it is!

Soup

4 large brown onions, sliced	6 egg yolks, beaten
½ cup olive oil	6 cups fish stock (see page 41)
pinch or sprig thyme	pinch cayenne pepper or a few drops
2 cloves garlic, crushed	tabasco sauce
2 tablespoons plain flour	juice of 1 lemon
½ bottle sauterne	60 g (2 oz) parmesan cheese, grated

Fish

gemfish or other thick white fish, boned and cut into portions of choice	pinch tarragon, chopped, or basil, fresh or dried
olive oil	pepper, freshly ground
juice of 1 lemon	salt

In a large saucepan, fry onions in olive oil until light brown. Add thyme, garlic and flour mixed to a paste with water and stir on a low flame for a few minutes. Add the wine and fish stock and simmer for ½ hour. Strain through a fine cloth or strainer.

Pour the strained soup into a clean pan, and just before you are ready to dine, make it hot and add the egg yolks, cayenne pepper or tabasco, lemon juice and parmesan cheese. Do not boil. Pour over cooked fish fillets and serve.

To cook fish, heat a little olive oil in a pan, add fish, lemon juice and other ingredients and lightly fry in olive oil until cooked. This should take only a few minutes if the fillets aren't too thick. Place carefully in a deep tureen and pour the bouillabaisse soup over them.

Serve with big chunks of crusty bread fried in olive oil.

NOTE: Gemfish is good in this one because, in season, it is economical. It is practically boneless and makes nice, thick fillets. But this bouillabaisse can also be made with other fish.

Serves 6

CRUNCHY FISH CHOWDER

I use gemfish for this dish because it is thick and easy to bone.

3 sticks celery, chopped

1 brown onion, chopped

1 small capsicum or ½ large pepper, chopped

2 tablespoons butter

1 teaspoon sugar

½ teaspoon dill

½ teaspoon basil

1 bay leaf, whole

3 drops tabasco sauce

pinch nutmeg

1 teaspoon salt

5 cups fish stock (see page 41)

1 kg (2 lb) or more thick fish fillets, boned and skinned, and chopped finely or cut into bite-size pieces

2 cups breadcrumbs, toasted in oven

butter

grated cheese

parsley, chopped

paprika

Place celery, onion and capsicum in a large, heavy pan and fry slowly in butter until soft, stirring all the time. Add seasonings, including sugar and tabasco sauce; mix all together and stir. Cook for a few minutes.

Add fish stock, mix all ingredients and cook for 5 minutes. Add the fish. Cook slowly 5 or 6 minutes. If you think there is too much stock in the mixture before you put the fish in, reduce the excess by fast boiling and then add the fish.

Turn all into a flat, shallow ovenproof dish and put breadcrumbs on top. Sprinkle with cheese, dot with butter and place under a hot grill to brown. Serve sprinkled with parsley and paprika.

Serve with hot garlic bread and creamy buttered potatoes, with a sprinkling of salad herbs.

NOTE: If there is oil floating on top of the chowder when made, that is OK. The toasted breadcrumbs absorb excess oil and the oil flavours the crumbs.

Serves 3–4

RICH VEGETABLE FISH CHOWDER

Chowders are generally a mixture of fish varieties, so if you have access to prawns, crayfish or crabs, by all means add them to this dish, to make it taste even better!

½ cup olive oil or polyunsaturated margarine or butter

1 brown onion, chopped

2 large sticks celery, chopped

1 capsicum, chopped

1 parsnip, chopped

1 carrot, chopped

½ leek, chopped

½ bunch shallots, chopped

1 clove garlic, chopped finely

½ teaspoon dill

basil

pinch nutmeg

dash tabasco sauce

salt and pepper

1 egg, beaten

1 kg (2 lb) or more thick fish (gemfish, jewfish, cod, etc.) filleted, boned and skinned, and cut into small portions

1 tablespoon fresh or canned cream

plain flour

Sao biscuit crumbs

1 cup moselle or fish stock (see page 41) sweetened with a little sugar

chopped parsley

paprika

Place ¼ cup oil in a very large pan and heat. Add vegetables and simmer slowly; add all seasonings and stir, turning vegetables over and over till mixed in. This will take about 15 minutes of slow cooking. Remove vegetables and leave until needed.

Coat fillets of fish with egg beaten with cream. Flour the fish, then dip in biscuit crumbs. Gently fry in remaining oil until fish is cooked, about 7 to 8 minutes, depending on thickness of fish.

Discard any oil left in pan. Pour wine or stock carefully around fish, boil fast for a couple of minutes without disturbing fish. Remove from heat and place crisp vegetables on top of fish. Warm through gently, garnish with parsley and paprika.

Serve with hot, fried bread croutons.

Serves 3

MICKY DRIP'S SEAFOOD CHOWDER

Served in winter at Fisherman's Wharf, Watson's Bay, this is Michael's speciality. Please order in advance if coming to eat at our place. Probably now that you know how to do it, we have lost a customer. Never mind, you will come back for something else in the seafood line, or just to gaze and dream a little, looking at Sydney Harbour.

Stock

2 fish heads or bones

1½ teaspoons salt

2 bay leaves

1 lemon, sliced

water

Chowder

1 kg (2 lb) fillets fresh fish, boned

125 g (4 oz) scallops

375 g (12 oz) prawns, shelled and deveined

1 small mud crab or 2 large blue swimmer crabs, cut up

1 large brown onion, chopped

1 or 2 sticks celery, chopped

1 cup potatoes, diced

2 large tomatoes, peeled and chopped

1 cup cream

2 cups milk

2 teaspoons curry powder

dash tabasco sauce

white pepper

1 dozen oysters (if feeling lavish)

parsley or celery tops, chopped

Make stock by putting fish heads or bones, salt, bay leaves and lemon into a large saucepan. Cover with water and bring to a boil. Simmer for 30 minutes. Strain bones, cool; remove any fish flesh from bones or head of fish, being careful you do not have any scales adhering. Discard bones. Put flesh aside for use in other dishes.

Return stock to clean pot and add fish, scallops, prawns. Simmer for ½ hour. Add onion, celery, potatoes, tomatoes. Add curry powder mixed with milk and cream. Stir in and cook a further 15 minutes. Season with pepper and tabasco. Just before ready to serve drop in oysters to warm through.

Garnish with parsley or celery tops.

Serve with fried bread croutons. People will do the Oliver Twist act for this one, and I reckon you will have to make more. It's very more-ish.

Serves 8

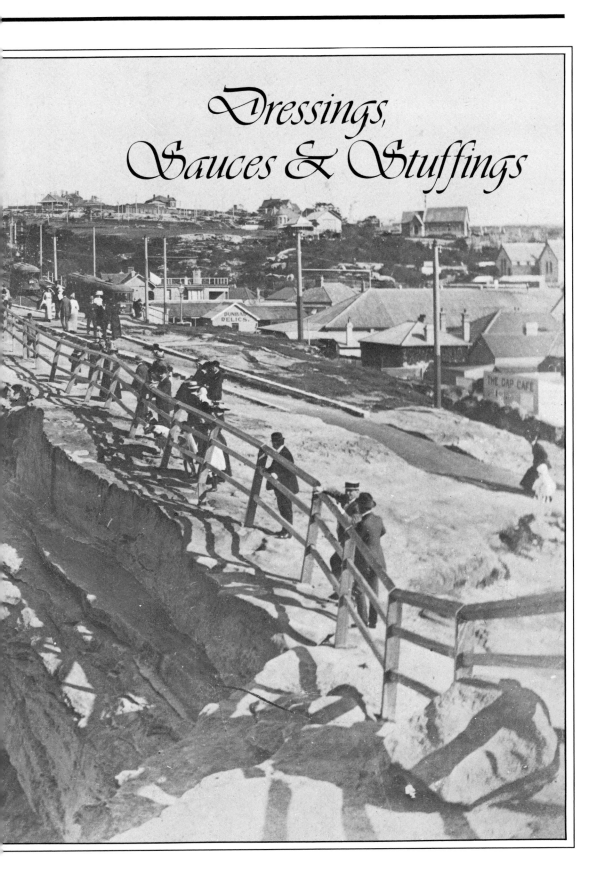

Dressings, Sauces & Stuffings

A good sauce can make simply cooked fish a gourmet meal. When you are deciding on a special dinner for friends and family, don't forget this. What could be nicer than freshly cooked, piping hot, grilled fish with a prawn or anchovy sauce, baked fish with oyster sauce, or even fried fish with home-made tartare sauce?

Thick fish fillets or steaks should always be served with a sauce, as they tend to be dry. A good sauce can be simply made by cooking tomatoes, onion and celery together with a few herbs and pepper and salt to your taste; or follow one of the recipes in this chapter. Serve the sauce in a separate jug or bowl, then everyone can have as much as he or she wants.

You will find the cocktail sauce useful, too, for when you have prawns at home.

BASIC MAYONNAISE

This is a delicious sauce and worth the effort.

1 cup olive or polyunsaturated oil (olive oil is best)

2 egg yolks

1 teaspoon mustard, made with mustard powder

1 teaspoon salt

½ teaspoon cayenne pepper

1 teaspoon caster sugar (or ordinary sugar)

2 dashes tabasco sauce

2 teaspoons vinegar

2 teaspoons tarragon vinegar

2 teaspoons lemon juice

Put the oil in a jug. Put aside.

Mix with a wooden spoon egg yolks, mustard, salt, cayenne pepper, sugar and tabasco sauce. Stir it around until you think it looks a bit "queer". Don't worry, keep stirring. While stirring, slowly add the oil drop by drop. (If you add the oil too quickly your mixture will curdle.) As you add the oil, you will notice it gets thicker and richer.

When all the oil is absorbed and you have a smooth coating consistency, add the vinegars slowly and then slowly add the lemon juice.

NOTE: You can add to this basic mayonnaise anything you choose. If your mixture curdles before you add the vinegars, etc., add drop by drop the beaten yolk of one more egg.

Makes about 1 cup

PREVIOUS PAGE: The famous Gap at Watson's Bay, early 1900s.

SIMPLE MAYONNAISE

1 teaspoon dry mustard

pinch cayenne pepper

1 teaspoon salt

½ teaspoon paprika

2 egg yolks

¼ cup brown vinegar

2 cups salad oil (preferably olive oil)

Place the mustard, cayenne pepper, salt, and paprika in a small bowl and mix together. Add the egg yolks and beat until creamy. Add half the brown vinegar and beat again. Add the oil gradually, a very small amount each time, until half the oil is used up. Then add the oil faster, 1 or 2 tablespoons at a time.

The mixture will thicken as you add all the oil. Beat in the rest of the vinegar, stirring it well into the mixture.

NOTE: Do not keep mayonnaise in a very cold part of the fridge. The oil will separate from the other ingredients.

EASY EGG YOLK DRESSING

I like tarragon vinegar best in this dressing.

2 egg yolks

1 teaspoon mustard

1 teaspoon caster sugar or ordinary sugar

freshly ground pepper

salt

300 ml (½ pint) fresh cream

vinegar, brown or white

dash paprika

Mix egg yolks, mustard, sugar, pepper and salt with some of the cream to a smooth consistency. Add vinegar to taste, then carefully add more cream until you reach the desired consistency. The mixture will thicken as it stands. Add paprika.

NOTE: Be careful of curdling when making this dressing. If the mixture does curdle, beat in another egg yolk, then add a little more cream.

FRENCH DRESSING

This is about the most popular dressing for avocados. I make it in a large jar which has a tight-fitting plastic lid. It can also be made in a cocktail shaker which has measurements.

1 cup olive or salad oil

1/3 cup tarragon or brown vinegar

1 clove garlic, crushed

1 teaspoon salad herbs

½ teaspoon paprika

freshly ground pepper

salt

Put all ingredients into your shaker, blender or jar and shake vigorously. Chill. Remove the garlic when ready to use. Shake each time you use it.

NOTE: If you like a sweeter dressing, add 1 teaspoon caster sugar.

SPICY DRESSING

This dressing is perfect to serve with avocados.

2 tablespoons tomato sauce, fresh, good quality

1 teaspoon French mustard

1 tablespoon horseradish, mixed

1 teaspoon worcestershire sauce

juice of 1 large lemon

pinch salt

Beat all ingredients together and use whenever needed.

Enough for two halves of an avocado

AVOCADO DRESSING

This dressing is used for side salads. Some like it for fish as well. You can use it with any meat dish or with any salad, or have it on the side as a sauce. Avocado dressing is a favourite of our customers. I make it in my food processor.

2 cloves garlic, crushed

1 teaspoon sugar

1 teaspoon dry mustard

1 teaspoon salad herbs

½ teaspoon dry dill (optional)

salt and pepper

3 drops tabasco sauce

1 small green capsicum

1 small red capsicum (with seeds)

2 sticks celery

2 large avocados

2 cups salad oil (olive oil is good)

⅓ cup tarragon vinegar

2 teaspoons malt vinegar

Blend together garlic, sugar, mustard, salad herbs, dill, pepper, salt and tabasco sauce. Add chopped capsicums and celery. Add flesh of avocados. Blend thoroughly for a few seconds. Add half the oil and vinegar while machine is running, then add the rest of the oil and vinegar together.

Carefully pour into jars and shake occasionally to distribute the mixture evenly.

NOTE: Keep this dressing in the fridge, but make sure it doesn't get too cold.

EGG SAUCE WITH CHIVES

A tasty addition to grilled, baked or fried fish.

3 eggs, hard-boiled, cold

2 or 3 tablespoons olive oil

½ teaspoon salt

1 tablespoon brown vinegar

1 teaspoon sugar

2 tablespoons chopped chives

Peel eggs and cut them in halves. Sieve the yolks and chop the whites finely. Mix with olive oil and salt, then add vinegar, sugar and chives.

TARTARE SAUCE

Tartare sauce in my opinion is used with seafoods far more than any other sauce. Here is a popular recipe which is easy to make.

2 cups mayonnaise

1 white onion, chopped

6 gherkins, chopped

1 stalk celery, chopped very finely

1 teaspoon chopped capers

1 teaspoon very finely chopped parsley

1 clove garlic, crushed and minced finely

1 tablespoon chopped chives

1 teaspoon tarragon vinegar

1 teaspoon red pimento (pepper)

dash of tabasco sauce

salt and pepper

To make a successful tartare sauce, the ingredients must be chopped very finely. You can use a blender for this if you wish.

Combine all ingredients together and bottle. Refrigerate, and use when needed with all seafoods.

NOTE: For variations on this sauce, add stuffed olives or well-drained spinach, chopped finely. This will make the sauce a green colour. Some people use artificial colouring in tartare sauce, but I think it is better to use vegetable juices.

GRANDFATHER'S FAVOURITE FISH SAUCE

So simple, and a nice sauce to serve with fried fish and chips. Sure to become a family favourite!

4 cups malt vinegar

2 tablespoons soy sauce

3 shallots, sliced

1 clove garlic

2 tablespoons walnut ketchup

3 drops tabasco sauce or pinch cayenne pepper

Place all ingredients in a large bottle and shake vigorously.

Date the bottle and put it in a cupboard. Shake every day for two weeks. Then divide into smaller bottles and store until ready to use.

NOTE: Walnut ketchup is obtainable at large delicatessens, or you can make it yourself when green walnuts are in season. Pickled walnuts may be substituted for the ketchup.

COCKTAIL SAUCE 1

This recipe is for all seafood dips and entrees. It is also excellent for fried prawns and for oysters. It even goes well with meat pies, frankfurts, sausage rolls and chips! This sauce is easy to make and tasty to eat.

½ cup mayonnaise

6 tablespoons tomato sauce

½ small can reduced cream

2 teaspoons worcestershire sauce

1 tablespoon brown vinegar or lemon

1 teaspoon horseradish sauce

freshly ground pepper

salt

pinch basil

parsley, chopped finely

dash tabasco sauce

Shake all ingredients thoroughly, or mix in a blender. Serve.

NOTE: Add crushed garlic if desired. Also, add some extra tomato sauce for chips and pies, etc.; this makes the sauce go further.

COCKTAIL SAUCE 2

1 small bottle tomato sauce

½ cup brown vinegar

1 small can reduced cream

1½ tablespoons worcestershire sauce

lemon juice

pinch of basil

salt and pepper

Shake or stir all ingredients until well mixed.

NOTE: Add garlic or other flavours if desired. If you are using this sauce immediately, use fresh instead of canned cream.

EPICUREAN SAUCE

¼ cup aspic jelly	1 teaspoon anchovy essence
1 cucumber	2 teaspoons gherkins, chopped
1 tablespoon tarragon vinegar	2 teaspoons chutney, chopped
½ cup mayonnaise	sugar to taste
¼ cup cream	salt and pepper to taste

Make aspic jelly by dissolving 2 teaspoons gelatine in ½ cup warm water. Let stand, but don't allow it to go too cold.

Peel cucumber thinly, cut into small pieces and cook until tender in salted water. Drain off water and rub cucumber through a sieve.

Mix cucumber puree with vinegar and aspic, which should be just lukewarm. Carefully mix mayonnaise with cream, anchovy essence, gherkins and chutney.

Blend both mixtures together. Season with salt, pepper and sugar and serve.

NOTE: A can of drained asparagus added to this sauce makes it very special.

SHAKA SAUCE

This is Grandfather's second-favourite sauce for his fish and chips. Grandma will enjoy it too.

4 cups malt vinegar	2½ tablespoons soy sauce
2 cloves garlic, chopped finely	2½ tablespoons mushroom ketchup
4 tablespoons walnut pickle or sauce	1½ tablespoons mango pickle

Place all ingredients in a large bottle and shake vigorously.

Date the bottle and put it in a cupboard. Shake 2 or 3 times daily (put the alarm on). At the end of a month this sauce will be ready to use.

NOTE: This sauce can be made only by stay-at-homes. It keeps for a good while in well-corked bottles. Walnut pickle or sauce may be unobtainable in your area, but you can make it yourself when green walnuts are in season.

MAÎTRE D'HÔTEL BUTTER

60 g (2 oz) butter, softened
1 teaspoon finely chopped parsley

1 teaspoon lemon juice
salt and pepper to taste

Mix all ingredients well. Spread on a plate and refrigerate. Use when required. Delicious on grilled or steamed fish.

ANCHOVY BUTTER

This is a tasty savoury spread or topping on grilled fish.

125 g (4 oz) butter
½ teaspoon anchovy essence or paste

pinch cayenne pepper
few drops cochineal or carmine

Mix all ingredients well. Be careful when adding colouring.
   This makes only a small amount of spread, enough for a few biscuits or 2 serves of fish.

LEGHORN SAUCE

This is an old-fashioned sauce for cold fish dishes and also for hot fillets of fish.

3 egg yolks, hard-boiled
vegetable oil or olive oil
3 anchovies, pounded or chopped
vinegar to taste

tarragon vinegar to taste
½ teaspoon finely chopped parsley
nutmeg to taste
pepper to taste

Crush egg yolks with a wooden spoon. Add oil, drop by drop at first, until the mixture is the consistency of thick cream. Stir in the rest of the ingredients.

NOTE: This sauce can be refrigerated until required.

HOT SAUCES

CLARIFIED BUTTER

This butter is sometimes called oiled or melted butter. It is often served instead of sauce with meat, fish and vegetables. It can also be used to moisten the surface of grilled food or dishes cooked au gratin, and for cooking instead of whole butter, giving excellent results.

Place butter in a small pan. Let it heat slowly, removing the scum as it rises. When the butter looks like clear salad oil, carefully pour it into a container, leaving the sediment at the bottom of the pan. Serve hot.

BUTTER SAUCE

Credit for this sauce goes to George Heydon, who once said: "My father used to tell me of a Murray Cod that was so big that it had to back up twice to get around the bend in the river." That really is a "big fish" yarn, George.

125 g (4 oz) butter
grated nutmeg
pinch each dill and basil
freshly ground pepper

salt
2 tablespoons plain flour
2 cups milk
juice of 1 lemon

Put butter and seasonings in a saucepan. Stir in flour. Add milk, stirring all the time, and simmer gently. Add lemon juice. Do not allow to boil. Serve immediately.

VEGETABLE SAUCE

My sister Flo's recipe for a sauce to go with her Old-fashioned Rissoles (page 141). Without the addition of a can of cream (see note), this is an excellent fat-free sauce for grilled or steamed fish.

1 small can tomatoes

1 onion, sliced and chopped

1 clove garlic, crushed (optional)

1 stick celery, chopped

½ red pepper, chopped

1 teaspoon sugar

pinch basil

salt and pepper

Put everything in a saucepan and boil rapidly until the juice of the tomatoes is reduced, i.e. until it is concentrated and thick.

NOTE: A small can of cream added to this sauce makes it really super. Also, a tablespoon of chutney is another variation. Chutney added later puts this into the upper class bracket!

FOUNDATION WHITE SAUCE

This is a smooth sauce for fish and shellfish. I often add to this basic sauce my favourite herbs and seasonings.

2 cups fish stock (see page 41)
* or milk, or a combination of both*

1½ tablespoons butter or margarine

2 tablespoons plain flour

freshly ground pepper

salt

dash of tabasco sauce

herbs or seasonings of choice

Place margarine or butter in a saucepan over a low flame and melt. Add flour and cook carefully for a few minutes, stirring, making sure no lumps form. Stir constantly to avoid burning or browning. Stir in gradually the fish stock or milk.

Boil gently for about 10 minutes until smooth and thick.

Foundation White Sauce with all its variations can be made in advance and reheated when ready to serve.

NOTE: When using this sauce for oysters, add a little worcestershire sauce to taste. Sometimes I add a finely chopped fresh celery stalk and a grated carrot to this sauce.

PLAIN FISH SAUCE

1 cup foundation white sauce (see page 61)
1 egg yolk

juice of 1 lemon or 1 teaspoon vinegar or
white wine

Make the foundation white sauce, add egg yolk but do not boil. Then add lemon juice, vinegar or white wine and simmer gently for a few minutes.

CHEESE SAUCE

2 tablespoons grated cheese
1 cup foundation white sauce (see page 61)
dash of ready-made mustard

To foundation white sauce add grated cheese and mustard. In this case, **do not boil.**

BECHAMEL SAUCE

This sauce should be very smooth. Work on it—you will master it in the end!

2 cups milk, or half milk and half fish stock
  (see page 41)
5 peppercorns
½ blade mace
1 small bay leaf
½ teaspoon dried herbs or a few sprigs
  fresh herbs

salt to taste
white roux paste made with 1 tablespoon butter,
  1 tablespoon flour
dash tabasco sauce

Heat milk or milk and fish stock in a saucepan with peppercorns, mace, bayleaf, herbs and salt. Simmer for about 15 minutes. Strain the seasonings from the milk.

Make the roux in a clean pan. Add the strained milk, stirring all the time. Boil gently for about 10 minutes. Season with pepper and salt and a dash of tabasco.

Pass this sauce through a very fine strainer.

SWEET AND SOUR SAUCE 1

This sauce is also very good with Pacific Platter (see page 146).

125 g (4 oz) can pineapple pieces, including liquid

2 stalks celery, strings removed and chopped

1 onion, sliced or cut in squares

1 carrot, sliced

½ red or green capsicum, chopped into strips or squares

1 cup water

2 pieces ginger in syrup, or ginger root, chopped finely

2 teaspoons golden syrup

1 tablespoon brown vinegar

juice from 1 can tomatoes

dash tabasco sauce

1 dessertspoon arrowroot

Put all ingredients except arrowroot in saucepan and cook slowly for 10 minutes. Dissolve arrowroot in a small quantity of water and thicken sauce with this, stirring for a few minutes until arrowroot is cooked.

Care must be taken not to cook vegetables until soft; they should retain some crispness.

SWEET AND SOUR SAUCE 2

½ cup vinegar, brown or tarragon

2 tablespoons brown sugar

1½ tablespoons soy sauce

½ can crushed pineapple (or 3 canned pineapple rings finely chopped)

2–3 pieces preserved ginger or ginger root, finely chopped

½ tablespoon arrowroot mixed with juice from canned pineapple

Put all ingredients except arrowroot in a saucepan and bring to the boil, cooking for a few minutes. Add arrowroot dissolved in a little water, stir until smooth and cook gently for about 10 minutes.

PARSLEY SAUCE

Very good with steamed fish, and a natural with smoked haddock or cod.

chopped parsley to taste
1 cup foundation white sauce (see page 61)

Add parsley to foundation white sauce.

CAPER SAUCE 1

A delicious, smooth sauce for all fish dishes.

1 tablespoon butter or margarine
2 tablespoons flour
about 1 cup fish stock (see page 41), boiling hot
2 tablespoons capers, chopped
liquid from capers

freshly ground pepper
salt
1 tablespoon cream
1 egg yolk (optional)

Melt butter or margarine in a deep saucepan, taking care it does not burn. Stir in the flour carefully. This will go into a ball. To mix to a smooth paste, gradually add the fish stock.

Add the chopped capers and a little of the liquid from the capers bottle and cook for about 10 minutes. Season with salt and pepper to taste. Stir constantly to get rid of any lumps of flour.

When the sauce is just about cooked, stir in cream. If you want to be lavish, add the egg yolk.

CAPER SAUCE 2

Thanks again to George Heydon. Serve this sauce with steamed or poached fish.

1 teaspoon anchovy sauce
2 or 3 tablespoons capers

¼ cup mushroom ketchup
dash chilli, vinegar or cayenne pepper

Mix all ingredients together.

ANCHOVY SAUCE

This sauce is simple to make and is very tasty with grilled fish.

3 anchovies (soaked overnight)
½ onion, chopped finely
parsley, chopped finely
2 tablespoons flour

1 tablespoon lard
water
salt, if required

Clean and chop finely the soaked anchovies. Discard soaking water. Add onion and parsley. Brown flour in lard, stirring, and then add anchovies and cook for only 1 minute.

Add water slowly, stirring, until required thickness is reached, then cook carefully for 15 minutes.

NOTE: Taste sauce before adding salt because anchovies are very salty. A tip: A good way of reducing the saltiness of anchovies is to soak them in milk for 20 to 30 minutes before using.

WHITE SAUCE FOR LOBSTER MORNAY OR THERMIDOR

An all-purpose white sauce (bechamel) to fill a 1 kg (2 lb) crayfish that is already cooked and split down the centre.

1 cup milk
1 cup fish stock (see page 41—but if you don't have fish stock, don't worry; instead of half milk, half stock, just use all milk mixed with a small amount of fresh cream)
1 small onion, chopped
1 bay leaf

pinch basil
60 g (2 oz) butter or margarine
1 tablespoon plain flour
½ cup grated tasty cheese
tabasco
paprika

Place milk and stock, onion, bay leaf and basil in a saucepan and let it simmer for about 20 minutes. Strain.

Melt butter in a saucepan, stir in the flour mixed with a little water to make a smooth paste.

Remove from heat, slowly add the strained milk, stirring all the time. Bring slowly to the boil, simmer 2 minutes.

Add grated cheese, a couple of drops of tabasco and a sprinkling of paprika.

YE OLD-FASHIONED PRAWN SAUCE

Serve over fish casseroles, grilled or steamed fish. You'll get plenty of praise for this one.

500 g (1 lb) cooked school prawns, peeled
1 cup foundation white sauce (see page 61)
½ teaspoon anchovy essence

cayenne pepper, to taste
few drops lemon juice

Use the shells and heads of the prawns to make the stock you will need for the foundation white sauce.

To heated white sauce add the prawns, anchovy essence, cayenne pepper and lemon juice. Cover the saucepan and let sauce cook on a low flame without boiling for a few minutes. Serve hot.

PACIFIC SEA SAUCE

1 250 g (8 oz) can or bottle tomato sauce
¼ cup chilli
1 teaspoon sugar
1 teaspoon worcestershire sauce

¼ teaspoon garlic powder
¼ teaspoon oregano
¼ teaspoon thyme
dash of basil

Combine all ingredients in a saucepan. Simmer for 10 to 12 minutes, stirring occasionally.

Makes about 1 large cup

ROUX PASTE

Roux is the French name for a paste used for thickening sauces, soups and gravies. The roux may be white, blond or brown, depending on how long it is cooked. White roux is used for white sauces. Roux paste is a rich foundation for any sauce.

Take equal quantities of butter and plain flour.
Melt butter, stir in flour. Cook, stirring, for a few minutes without browning.
If a blond or brown roux is required, cook for a little longer until colour deepens.

CURRY SAUCE

Serve this sauce on top of Pacific Platter (see page 146) or baked, fried, steamed or grilled fish.

2 tablespoons butter or margarine

1 large brown onion, chopped

2 sticks celery, strings removed and chopped

500 g (1 lb) ripe tomatoes

1 medium-sized can of tomatoes

1 small capsicum (green pepper) or ½ large capsicum

2 teaspoons curry powder (or to taste)

2 bay leaves, crushed

½ teaspoon basil

½ teaspoon pepper

½ teaspoon salt

2 teaspoons sugar

grated rind of 1 lemon

juice of 1 lemon

dash tabasco sauce

juice from canned tomatoes or water

In a large frying pan, melt butter and brown onion (do not burn) and cook slowly. Add celery, drained canned tomatoes (reserve liquid), chopped fresh tomatoes, capsicum, garlic, curry powder, bay leaves, basil, pepper and salt.

Cook for 10 minutes over a medium heat. Add sugar, lemon, tabasco and tomato juice or water to make quantity and thickness required. Heat through.

NOTE: You can add extra vegetables to this sauce, if you like. Cream can be added as well, and instead of water you can use white wine.

HOLLANDAISE SAUCE

This is a favourite of mine. It is rich, and I always add some of my favourite
herbs to dress it up.

*1 cup foundation white sauce or bechamel sauce
(see page 61 or 62)*

*1 to 4 egg yolks, depending on quantity of
sauce required*

milk or fish stock (see page 41)

lemon juice

cayenne pepper

salt

pinch basil or nutmeg

Heat your sauce slowly.

Beat the egg yolks with a little milk or stock. (If you are making a large quantity of sauce,
add each yolk separately.) Add to the sauce and stir over a low flame until cooked and thick.
Add lemon juice, cayenne, salt, and basil or nutmeg.

If you think the sauce is too thick, add more stock or milk to make the consistency required.

NOTE: Sometimes I add a small amount of mustard or a dash or two of tabasco to this sauce.

TASTY SAUCE FOR SMOKED FISH

Credit for this sauce goes to George Heydon.

roux paste

milk in which smoked fish has been poached

seasoning to taste

hard-boiled eggs, chopped

cucumber, chopped

Make a roux paste, using plain flour or cornflour. Add milk and seasoning to taste, then eggs
and cucumber.

Pour the sauce over the fish, and serve.

STUFFINGS

STUFFING FOR FISH 1

Stuff the inside of a fish with this and sew up the opening. This stuffing is
suitable for smaller fish, which cook quickly.

90 g (3 oz) breadcrumbs

60 g (2 oz) butter

*2 anchovies, canned (optional), or salt
  to taste*

6 tablespoons cream or milk

2 egg yolks

1 dozen oysters, chopped

Blend or thoroughly mix breadcrumbs, butter and anchovies. Add the cream or milk and the
egg yolks.

Put the mixture in a saucepan and heat and stir the mixture until it thickens, which should
take about 5 minutes. Remove from heat. Add oysters and mix well.

STUFFING FOR FISH 2

Here is another stuffing for good measure. After all, that large fish Dad caught or
won in a raffle deserves the best. The mixture can be used as a filling for a whole
fish or it can be served on top of baked fillets of fish, when it should be placed
over the fish 10 minutes before the end of the cooking time.

60 g (2 oz) butter

1 tablespoon plain flour

1 cup milk or fish stock (see page 41)

2 eggs

salt and pepper

*500 g (1 lb) raw fish (cod, salmon, gemfish
  are ideal), boned*

Melt butter, stir in flour, add milk or fish stock and cook until mixture is a compact mass around
the bowl of the spoon. Add eggs one by one, beat in well. Season well with salt and pepper,
then pass mixture through a wire sieve.

Add chopped fish, and mix well.

A lighter mixture can be obtained when required by blending or pounding 3 eggy yolks
with the fish and mixing in 3 egg whites, whipped until they are stiff. Do this after passing
the mixture through a sieve.

Seafood

Once upon a time "seafoods" just meant oysters, prawns, crabs and lobsters to most people. But these days, largely thanks to influences from Europe and Asia, a large range of shellfish, crustaceans and other creatures are appearing in our fishmarkets: scallops, mussels, pippies, abalone, "Balmain bugs", squid, octopus, cuttlefish and more are all becoming more and more popular. In this section of the book you'll find good recipes for a wide range of seafoods, and at the end three recipes which are really "seafood extravaganzas", using several different kinds of seafoods: Doyle's Paella, Seafood Bonanza and Peking Firepot.

The most important thing to remember when cooking seafoods is not to overcook. The flesh is delicate and needs to be cooked quickly and removed from the heat straight away — not simmered until it is tough and stringy. And don't overpower the fresh, delicate flavour of shellfish and crustaceans by using strong sauces and seasonings — the natural subtle taste of the fresh seafood will carry the dish, if you let it.

PREVIOUS PAGE: *Hornby Lighthouse at the entrance to Sydney Harbour, 1900.*

PRAWNS

As soon as prawns are mentioned, so is that old Australian saying "Don't come the raw prawn". So I certainly won't. These are all "yummy" recipes, and if you are using cooked prawns I think you had better have twice the quantity you need for your recipe unless you can find someone who is allergic to eating them to peel them for you. I'm a hopeless case myself—one for the pot and one for my mouth! When you do come the "raw prawn", that's a different matter—I mean the "green", uncooked prawn, with which so many dishes are made. They're harder to shell and devein, but they give delicious results.

How many of you have been prawning? Whenever it was or will be, it is one of the happiest times of your life. A great spot in New South Wales for prawning is Tuggerah Lakes, not so far from Sydney. I just love that place. To me it means Christmas time and the school holidays, sharing houses, work done in a jiffy, Mums, Dads and the kids fishing, strolling, surfing, calm ankle-depth water for the littlies, and the smell of hot fish and chips everywhere. And prawns—no Lakes holiday is complete without that magic word. What's a mosquito or two on those hot, dark nights in the stillness of the lake when the prawns are running? And then home, all talking at once, with wet clothes, shivering too, happiness everywhere, big pots of boiling water ready for the night's catch, television forgotten, and the art of conversation returned for a little while.

Freshly caught prawns—a feast!

COOKING GREEN PRAWNS

Just say we have 1 kg (2 lb) of freshly caught prawns. (You may have lots more—I hope you do.) If the prawns are alive, put them into fresh water first and they will "bring up" any sand, etc.

Have a big saucepan ready with about 2½ litres (5 pints) of water and bring to the boil; throw in a handful (about 2 tablespoons) of common cooking salt—the good, old-fashioned salt. Please do not use table salt. The salt helps to preserve the prawns if they are not to be eaten straight away, and retains the heat of the boiling water. Small school prawns should be cooked in 3 minutes, the larger prawns in 4 minutes. To be sure, make a test: the prawns will come to the top of the water and float, which is a good indication that they are nearly done. Take out a prawn and hold it to the light. If it is cooked, you will see that the flesh has shrunk from the shell slightly, and the prawn looks translucent. Be careful not to undercook your prawns— you will know if you have because they will get a black look on part of the body when cold. As soon as you are sure the prawns are done, remove them from the boiling water and place in a big bowl of iced water, to cool them.

Now they're ready to peel, devein and eat with vinegar or lemon and bread and butter, or in salads, fried rice, curry and all the other dishes that call for cooked prawns. Don't forget to keep the prawn heads and shells to make stock (see recipe for fish stock, page 41).

AUSTRALIAN AVOCADO AND PRAWNS

Here in Australia we have some of the best prawns in the world — many of them
swimming in my beautiful Sydney Harbour. And in the Sunshine State grow delectable
avocados — soft, nutty and delicious.
What a double!

16 large, cooked prawns, peeled	*paprika*
4 small, cupped lettuce leaves	*thin lemon wedges*
2 ripe avocados	*thin tomato wedges*
French dressing	*parsley sprigs*

Put 4 prawns aside for garnish. Chop remaining prawns and put aside.

Take 4 individual serving dishes and put a lettuce leaf in each one.

Wash avocados and dry. Split in two lengthwise and remove the seeds. Put one avocado
half into each lettuce cup. Pour dressing into the centre where the seed has been and grind over
a little black pepper and salt.

Fill the avocado centres with prawns, pour over more French dressing then top each serving
with one of the whole prawns kept aside.

Sprinkle with paprika, and decorate dishes with lemon and tomato wedges, and a parsley
sprig or two.

Serves 4 as an entree

PRAWN SALAD WITH AVOCADO DRESSING

How we all love avocados, and how lavish we feel when we are able to serve them to our family or friends. A couple of avocados can go a long way when made into a puree to be used as a spread or dressing. Here is my recipe for avocado puree, here used as a dressing for prawn salad. It would go just as well with a plain vegetable salad.

1 kg (2 lb) cooked prawns, peeled
lettuce cups, tomato, spring onions, cucumber and any other ingredients you care to add

For the avocado dressing

2 avocados
grated rind and juice of 1 lemon
freshly ground pepper and salt
1 onion, grated

¼ teaspoon paprika
1 tablespoon olive oil
½ teaspoon tarragon vinegar

Wash the avocados and dry. Cut in half lengthwise, remove seed. Scoop flesh out into basin, mash a little with a silver fork or wooden spoon. Add grated rind and juice of lemon, pepper and salt, onion, paprika and vinegar. Mix.

Beat in olive oil with a wooden spoon, or puree mixture in a blender. Cover and refrigerate until needed. This makes 3 cups of puree.

Put lettuce cups on plates and fill with prawns. Arrange other salad ingredients attractively around prawns.

Serve salads with dressing poured over, or in a separate bowl so that guests can help themselves.

Serves 6

As large king prawns are becoming so popular now in Australia, and new prawning grounds are being searched for, the demand for prawns far exceeds the supply at times. The most popular prawn dish in our restaurants at present is Stuffed Prawns with the most delicious "dip" sauce. When the prawns are eaten, you can mop up the rest of the sauce with the remains of your bread roll. Filling, but oh so more-ish. Fattening, of course, but tomorrow you starve. So when the large green prawns are in season, treat yourself and the family. You all deserve it.

STUFFED GREEN KING PRAWNS
with a luxury filling and sauce

You will try to do an Oliver Twist act with this one, for sure.

24 large green king prawns, raw
oil for frying
beer batter (see page 84)

Filling
6 slices thick bacon
1 tin spinach
1 large egg
1 onion
butter
1 clove garlic, crushed
parsley
breadcrumbs
pinch salt
½ cup sultanas, soaked in wine and drained

Sauce
1 small jar fruit chutney
1 tablespoon curry powder
6 fine shallots, chopped
1 small jar mayonnaise
1 egg white, beaten

Butterfly the prawns by cutting each one down to the start of the tail and gently flattening both sides. Devein and remove the heads.

Remove bacon rinds and chop bacon finely. Drain the spinach well. Chop the onion and fry lightly in butter with the garlic. Mix the filling ingredients together, using enough breadcrumbs to bind. Fill the cut section of the butterfly prawns with the mixture, press the sides firmly together and set aside in the refrigerator for a while to firm.

Prepare the sauce by blending all ingredients together carefully, adding the egg white last. Serve in a large bowl or individual dishes.

When you are ready to cook, dip stuffed prawns carefully in the batter, and fry in your favourite cooking oil (mine is olive oil) for 5 minutes in a deep pan. Remember to have the oil hot, but not at boiling point or the prawns will cook outside first.

Serve with the delicious fruity curry sauce.

Serves 6

PINEAPPLE PRAWNS

2 tablespoons vegetable oil

1 brown onion, chopped finely

1 teaspoon salt

freshly ground pepper

2 large stalks celery, strings removed and
    chopped finely

½ capsicum (green pepper), chopped finely

1 cup tomato sauce

1 cup canned crushed pineapple

1–1.5 kg (2–3 lb) cooked prawns, shelled

Heat oil in a large pan, add onion and cook until tender, being careful not to burn the oil. Add the salt and pepper, celery, capsicum, tomato sauce and pineapple, stir well. Bring to the boil, then reduce heat and simmer for about 5 minutes.

Add the prawns, mix well, and heat through, remembering that the prawns are already cooked.

Serve over a bed of rice.

Serves 3–4

SYDNEY HARBOUR PRAWNS

1–1.5 kg (2–3 lb) cooked prawns, shelled

4 tomatoes, chopped

250 g (½ lb) button mushrooms

½ cup warm white sauce (see page 61)

25 g (4 oz) butter

½ teaspoon cayenne pepper

1 teaspoon salt

1 teaspoon mustard

parsley

Put the prawns, tomatoes and mushrooms through a hand mincing machine or blender, or chop together very finely. If using a blender, be careful not to blend too long—just a few seconds will do.

Put mixture in saucepan with white sauce and other ingredients, except parsley. Allow to come to boil; simmer for 5 minutes.

Serve over rice or noodles, and garnish with parsley.

Serves 4

CURRIED PRAWNS IN THE OLD-FASHIONED WAY

1.5 kg (3 lb) cooked prawns, shelled (reserve shells and heads)

2 tablespoons butter or olive oil

3 large onions, chopped

4 small cloves garlic, chopped

1 tablespoon curry powder

salt and freshly ground pepper

4 large sticks celery, chopped finely

2 small capsicums, seeded and chopped

4 tomatoes, chopped, or 1 small can tomatoes, drained

2 teaspoons sugar

1 bay leaf, crushed

½ teaspoon basil

1 tablespoon tomato paste

2 cups stock made by cooking the prawn shells and heads in salted water or tomato juice or wine or water

grated rind and juice of 2 lemons

chopped parsley

Make stock with prawn shells and heads (see page 41).

In a heavy pan melt butter or oil, add onions and garlic and fry until a pale golden colour.

Add curry powder, pepper and salt, celery, capsicums, tomatoes, sugar, bay leaf, basil and tomato paste. Cook slowly over a medium heat for 15 minutes.

Stir in stock, add peeled prawns and warm through. Do not cook the prawns or the dish will be spoilt. When dish is hot, stir through lemon rind and juice.

Serve the curried prawns on a bed of fluffy rice or with lots of fresh, crisply cooked vegetables, hot rolls or toast fingers. Garnish with parsley.

Serves 4–6

FISHERMAN'S WHARF GARLIC PRAWNS

Michael's special garlic prawn recipe—and a wizard at cooking it is his son Jim at our Fisherman's Wharf Restaurant, Watson's Bay. I think Jim's had a few burnt fingers in his time, but then, who can resist a hot garlic prawn? Well, here is the recipe. You can use it for an entree or a main dish. It may sound like too much garlic and pepper, but no, the result will please you.

4 cloves garlic

½ teaspoon salt

2 teaspoons black peppercorns, crushed coarsely

2 teaspoons lemon juice

1 tablespoon brandy

500 g (1 lb) green prawns, shelled, cleaned and split lengthwise

olive oil

chopped parsley

½ cup cream

Crush garlic with salt, add crushed peppercorns, lemon juice and brandy. Mix well.

Place prawns in saucepan or in those heavy, individual iron dishes you can now buy to cook and serve garlic prawns in. Add garlic mixture and enough olive oil to just cover and cook quickly until prawns just change colour. Stir in cream.

Serve hot and sizzling in small bowls garnished with chopped parsley.

Serves 4 as an entree, 2 as a main course

PRAWNS À LA EVANS HEAD

My friend Nell from Evans Head sent me this recipe, and she says it is delicious with a bottle of old red.

125 g (4 oz) butter

juice of 2 lemons

500 g (1 lb) cooked prawns

1 teaspoon anchovy sauce

2½ cups white sauce (see page 61)

lemon slices

Melt the butter in a pan with the lemon juice and then add the prawns and anchovy sauce. Allow to stand in a warm place for 30 minutes until a nice pink colour. (The lemon draws the colour from the prawns.)

Stir in the warm white sauce and add cayenne pepper to taste. Allow to boil, stirring, simmer for 2 minutes and serve very hot on toast with slices of lemon.

Serves 2

PETER DOYLE'S PRAWN CUTLETS

Delicious prawn cutlets as served at Doyle's on the Beach Restaurant, Watson's Bay. Customers keep coming back for more. This is Peter's own recipe, which he often uses at home, as well as at work.

1 kg (2 lb) green prawns
pepper and salt
flour

water
oil for deep-frying
lemon wedges or cocktail sauce (see page 57)

The time-consuming part of making prawn cutlets is the preparation beforehand. Cut or pull off heads. Shell, being careful not to remove tail. Split prawns down back and devein. Wash and pat dry.

Open prawns out and flatten, using the flat side of a cleaver, a rolling pin or a broad-bladed knife. Season the prawns with pepper and salt and refrigerate, covered, until ready to cook.

Make a very fresh batter of just plain flour, adding cold water slowly and beating until you have a thin, runny batter, just like pancake batter.

Heat oil in a deep saucepan or fryer, which should be at least half full. Dip the prawns in the batter and add to oil, a few at a time. The prawns come straight up to the surface, and in a couple of minutes they are cooked. Drain well.

Serve straight away with lemon wedges or, as we do, a creamy, freshly made cocktail sauce.

Nothing to it—no secret batters, just very fresh batter, good prawns, the best of cooking oil and cooked to order, not reheated.

Serves 4 as an entree, 2 as a main course

PRAWNS SUPREME

This may seem to be just plain fried prawn cutlets, rice and vegetables. Yes, it is—with a difference, though. It is the extra care you take in the preparation, the frying oil, the batter, in using green prawns, in the slightly crunchy vegetables.

1 kg (2 lb) large green prawns, shelled
(It doesn't really matter if they are small;
they just take longer to shell and devein.)

1 egg beaten in 2 tablespoons cream

plain flour seasoned with pepper and salt

2 cups cooked rice

2 tablespoons butter

4 cloves garlic, crushed, or a pinch dried basil

2 brown onions, chopped finely

4 large sticks celery, strings removed and
chopped finely

1 small or ½ large green capsicum (pepper),
washed, seeded and chopped finely

½ teaspoon tabasco

olive oil

parsley, chopped finely

lemon wedges

Split prawns down centre of back and remove vein. Flatten a little if prawns are large and thick. Dip prawns in egg and cream mixture and toss in flour. Put on a plate, cover and put in fridge until ready to cook.

Put cooked rice in a colander, cover with a damp cloth and place over saucepan of gently boiling water to reheat.

In a saucepan melt butter over a low heat. Add garlic, onions, celery, capsicum, pepper and salt and tabasco, mix well and cook slowly for about 12 minutes, when vegetables should still be fairly crisp. Keep warm but do not cook further.

Heat olive oil in a shallow pan, add prawns and fry over a medium heat for 5 to 10 minutes, according to size and thickness, until golden brown. Drain well.

Serve on very hot plates, using the rice as a foundation, flattened on plate. Pile green vegetable mixture on top and put the prawns in the centre. Garnish with finely chopped parsley, or any green garnish you may have, and plenty of lemon wedges. This can be eaten as an entree or as a main meal, with soy sauce or sweet and sour sauce (see page 63) as desired.

Serves 4

ALICE'S PAN-FRIED PRAWN CUTLETS

24 large green prawns
2 eggs
4 tablespoons cream
¼ teaspoon tabasco
pinch basil
plain flour seasoned with pepper and salt

about 16 Sao biscuits rolled out to make crumbs
olive oil
lemon wedges
parsley
cocktail sauce (see page 57) (optional)

Prepare the prawns as for Peter Doyle's Prawn Cutlets (see page 80).

Beat eggs, cream, tabasco and basil together on a large dinner plate. Spread paper on your work bench and put the seasoned flour on one part and the Sao biscuit crumbs on another. Dip the prawns first in flour, then in egg and cream, and finally in the biscuit crumbs.

In a large, heavy frying pan, put enough olive oil to cover the base. Heat. Add prawns and fry over a medium heat, first on one side, then on the other, for about 10 minutes, until golden.

Drain and serve very hot on hot plates and garnish with lemon wedges and parsley. Serve plain or with creamy cocktail sauce.

Serves 4 as an entree, 2 as a main course

JOHN DOYLE'S MILD MUSTARD PRAWNS

An impressive main-course dish from Doyle's on the Beach at Rainbow Bay, Coolangatta. (See page 105 for John's Oysters Supreme entree.) This recipe gives the quantities for 1 kg large green prawns. You can adjust quantities according to the number of prawns you wish to serve per person.

1 kg (2 lb) large green prawns, gutted, cleaned and headed

150 g (5 oz) butter

1 tablespoon pure olive oil

1 tablespoon finely chopped white onion

½ teaspoon chopped garlic

1 teaspoon Dijon mustard

1 teaspoon chopped fresh herbs (basil, dill, oregano, or your own choice—if using dried herbs, use only a pinch of each)

½ cup brandy

½ cup cream

freshly ground black pepper

salt (if needed)

Cut cleaned prawns down the centre and open out butterfly-style, leaving the tail intact.

Melt half of butter and oil in a deep pan; add prawns, onion, garlic, mustard, herbs, pepper and salt (if used). Cook over medium heat for 8 to 10 minutes, according to size and thickness of prawns.

Add brandy to pan; flame. Add cream, then thicken with remaining butter.

Serve immediately on very hot plates, garnished with sprigs of parsley and/or fennel, and accompany with a crisp salad or wild rice.

SCAMPI

Scampi and prawns (or shrimps) are two different crustaceans. True scampi are small members of the lobster family, with very thin and meatless nippers. These large scampi are caught off the continental shelf of Australia in very deep water.

Care must be taken when cooking scampi, as the meat will break down and become soft with overcooking. Although they provide a small quantity of meat, what is there is just so delicious. After eating large scampi, you may like to dry the skeletons and have them as fragile "decorations", varnished for the mantelpiece (that's if you have a mantelpiece).

These scampi recipes are the ones our son John uses in his restaurant. I will leave the quantity of scampi you use to your own discretion.

DEEP-FRIED SCAMPI TAILS

scampi
oil for frying

Beer Batter

2 large cups plain flour
1 can beer

1 teaspoon salt
2 egg whites, lightly beaten

To prepare the batter, put flour in a deep basin and add the beer slowly. Add salt, mix to a smooth, thin batter, and then add the egg whites. You may have to add a little more flour at this stage — the batter has to be well mixed and kept thin, yet retain "body".

Split scampi tails, flatten lightly, and coat them in the beer batter. Fry in fresh clean oil for 3 to 4 minutes.

CHILLED SCAMPI

scampi
olive oil
1 large red chilli, chopped

salt
chopped garlic
paprika

Split the scampi by cutting carefully down the centre to the tail, leaving the head intact. Devein with a sharp knife and clean.

Lay the scampi in a baking dish and pour over enough olive oil to cover. Add the chopped red chilli, and sprinkle with cooking salt, a liberal helping of chopped garlic and some fresh paprika.

Decrease a preheated oven to 150°C (300°F) and bake for 15 minutes. When cooked, leave scampi in the baking dish and serve chilled in the natural juice they were baked in.

HOT BAKED SCAMPI

scampi
clarified butter (see page 60)
1 teaspoon mustard powder
olive oil

chillies
chopped garlic, to taste
1 cup chablis (or other white wine)

Split the scampi by cutting carefully down the centre from head to tail, and clean.

Place all other ingredients in a saucepan and bring slowly to the boil. Remove from heat, pour liquid into a flat baking dish and carefully place scampi in the dish. (This may be done hours before you are ready to cook.) Decrease a preheated oven to 150°C (300°F) and bake for 15 minutes.

The "eye appeal" improves if you bake a long red chilli with the scampi and serve it on the side of the dish.

CRAB

At one time we had a huge tank of salt water in which we used to keep some huge crabs alive, in the dining room of our old hotel. They were fascinating to watch — especially at feeding time, when they really used to have stand-up fights over the fresh green prawns. It wasn't a selection tank, though it was large enough for it. It was just for the customers to see, and the children were always amused by it. It was a lot of work keeping the water clear and bringing up salt water from the Bay, so eventually we put the crabs in buckets and took them down to the water's edge at Watson's Bay under the wharf, where they remained for a few days, and then they probably went out to sea with the tides to regain their strength. They were like your old pet duck or "chook" to us; we could never have eaten them or served them to anyone else. Later on we used the big tank at our Wharf Restaurant at Watson's Bay, where it held an assortment of local fish. The children who fished down the wharf, including all our children, would come and "sell" the tiddlers to us for the tank . . . it was fun.

I've had lots of fun with live crabs in my time, although when we have the mud crabs brought down from Queensland they are transported and securely tied with rope. Some of them weigh up to 2.5 kg (5 lb), and being very much alive, you can just imagine the "nip" they can give you (I mean the full measure, not half a "nip"). Once, years ago, I had some smaller ones in the restaurant, and my young son undid the string and, much to the amazement and surprise of the customers, and my horror, let them go, to roam around where they pleased. You can imagine the laughter — and the time I had catching them.

COOKING BLUE SWIMMER CRABS

Blue swimmer crabs usually die very quickly after being caught, so you must, if possible, cook them immediately.

When ready to cook, place crabs in boiling, salted water and bring back to boil. Cook, simmering, for 10 minutes.

Place in cold water to cool down. Serve with bread and butter and lemon, or your favourite sauce.

Another good way of cooking blue swimmers is to cut them in two, dip halves into batter and deep-fry. Drain well and serve with lemon or cocktail sauce (see page 57).

COOKING A LIVE MANGROVE CRAB

1 live mangrove crab, about 1 kg (2 lb)
salt
water

When you buy the crab, it will probably be tied together with string to keep those nippers from nipping you. Place the live crab in the coolest part of the refrigerator (not the freezer.) Crabs come from warmer waters of Australia and the cold makes them fall into a deep, final sleep. This should take from 2 to 3 hours, and then the crab is ready to cook.

Fill a large boiler with enough water to cover the crab. Bring to the boil. Add a large handful of salt — butcher's salt or your plain ordinary cooking salt, not table salt.

Place the crab in water, bring the water back to the boil, then turn down heat so crab simmers slowly for about 20 minutes. When cooked, cool crab in a tub of cold water, otherwise it will keep cooking in the heat retained inside the shell.

Larger crabs will, of course, take a little longer to cook — use your own judgment here.

One 1 kg (2 lb) crab will usually serve 2 people

PREPARING CRAB FOR SALAD

Slip a knife under the shell at the back of the crab and lift shell from body. Clean out waste under a running tap. Careful, otherwise you will wash the flavour out of the crab. Some people I have seen eat the roe and fat part from the head, others discard these.

Crack claws with a wooden mallet or small hammer.

With a sharp knife, cut crab in half or quarters, remembering to keep head shell for decoration.

To serve, arrange crab in its original shape, on a large plate lined with lettuce.

The crab can be served alone, with bread and butter, or with a side salad or well-minted hot potato salad. A pair of nutcrackers or crab crackers, and a couple of long steel skewers to draw the last piece of meat from the legs, are helpful. So is a large bowl to collect the bits and pieces of shell as the meal progresses.

One large crab serves 2

CRAB MORNAY

1 large mud crab, cooked, or frozen crab   *2 tablespoons warm white sauce (see page 61)*

2 tablespoons butter   *mashed potato (optional)*

1 tablespoon chopped shallots   *grated cheese*

freshly ground black pepper   *fine brown breadcrumbs (optional)*

pinch basil   *parsley*

½ cup white wine

Remove the meat from the crab (see page 87), or allow frozen crab to thaw naturally.
Heat 1 tablespoon butter in a pan, add shallots and fry gently. Add pepper, basil and the crab meat, heat through gently. Be careful not to overcook.

Add wine and white sauce, mix well, reheat.

Pour mixture over a base of dry, buttered mashed potatoes, in an ovenproof dish. Alternatively, omit mashed potatoes, and place crab mixture in scallop shells or ramekins. Top with remaining butter, in dabs, and grated cheese mixed, if you like, with some fine brown breadcrumbs.

Place dish under griller for a few minutes to brown cheese.

Decorate with parsley and serve.

Serves 2 as a main course, 4 as an entree

STUFFED DEVILLED CRABS

This recipe is courtesy of Mrs John R. Davis, wife of a former US Consul-General here in Sydney. It really is a super-delicious American crab dish. Thank you, Mrs Davis.

500 g (1 lb) crab meat, flaked	*½ clove garlic, crushed*
4 tablespoons lime juice	*1 teaspoon chopped parsley*
2 teaspoons onion pulp	*¼ teaspoon dry mustard*
1 teaspoon black pepper	*pinch basil*
2 dashes tabasco	*pinch mace*
salt	*2 tablespoons light rum*
3 tablespoons butter	*2 tablespoons fine breadcrumbs*
2 tablespoons chopped onion	*cracker crumbs*
2 tablespoons chopped capsicum (green pepper)	*parmesan cheese*
1 small tomato, chopped	

Mix the crab, lime juice, onion, pepper, tabasco and salt and let stand, covered, in the refrigerator for a couple of hours.

Melt 2 tablespoons butter in a pan, add onion, capsicum, tomato, garlic and parsley and fry gently until soft. Add mustard, basil, mace, rum and breadcrumbs and stir over a gentle heat for 2 minutes.

Add marinated crab to mixture in pan and heat through, stirring well, for about 5 minutes.

Place mixture in cleaned crab shells or ramekins, sprinkle with cracker crumbs mixed with an equal amount of parmesan cheese, dot with remaining butter and bake in a medium oven for 5 minutes.

Serves 2 as a main course, 4 as an entree

CURRIED CRAB

1 large cooked crab or frozen crab
2 tablespoons butter
1 small brown onion, chopped finely
2 teaspoons curry powder
pinch basil

about 1 cup white sauce (see page 61) or
    crab stock plus about 1 tablespoon cornflour
    mixed to a paste with cold milk
salt and pepper
desiccated coconut
lemon wedges

Crack crab and remove meat (see Preparing Crab for Salad, page 87), or allow frozen crab to thaw naturally. If you like, boil the shells with water to make stock.

Melt butter in a pan, add onion and fry gently until tender. Add curry powder, basil and white sauce or well-strained stock. If using stock, thicken mixture with a little cornflour made into paste with cold milk. The amount of liquid you will need depends on the size of the crab, so use your own judgment. Add salt and pepper to taste.

Do not overcook, remembering that the crab has already been cooked. Just heat through. Serve on a bed of boiled rice, garnished with lemon wedges and desiccated coconut.

Serves 2

LOBSTER

We in Australia are lucky to have an abundance of crayfish (usually called lobsters here) in the sea surrounding our continent, and they are big dollar earners for our country, being exported overseas, mostly from Western Australia. Most states have their own local species, which can be identified by shell markings. Some have a very rough, spiky outer shell and when cooked are a very bright red. Others, like the ones that come from the areas around New South Wales, are smoother, and paler when cooked.

When selecting your crayfish (or lobster, whichever you like), remember that size for size, the female of the species has much more meat than the male, so it is heavier and the flesh is sweeter too (only natural, being a female — now, now boys!). To tell a female? Well, look on the underside of the tail; you will notice that the females' fins are longer than those of the males, and touch each other. Also, the back legs have a little "finger and thumb" with which the female places her eggs in crevices and under rocks and seaweed.

Have you ever heard that yarn about the kids buying chocolate boys and girls (in my time they were about a penny each) and little Eva saying: "Mummy, I want a boy chocolate, because you get a bit extra."

In the crayfish line, the female has it!

COOKING A GREEN LOBSTER

To kill the crayfish (I always hated to do it and used to say, "Please, God, don't let it feel any pain"), place it in a tub or large basin of fresh cold water until drowned. If your green crayfish is already dead, please make sure it is very fresh.

Place a good handful of common cooking salt — not table salt — in a big pot of boiling water. Cut up and add lemon, if available, a large onion, a stick of celery, carrot — then in goes the crayfish. This crayfish water makes good stock for all seafood dishes. If you just want the crayfish cooked and do not need stock, just add a handful of white sugar with the salt and forget about putting in the vegetables.

A 1 kg (2 lb) crayfish should take altogether about 15 to 20 minutes' gentle boiling. If you have only a kitten-size crayfish, 12 minutes will be enough. Remember that crayfish lose weight when boiled, and overcooking will toughen and cause greater weight loss.

Lift crayfish out with tongs and bend the tail backwards and forwards. It should be pliable and return to the curled position. Place crayfish in cool running water.

Well, that's how it's done, though I suppose you will probably mostly buy your cooked crayfish (lobster) from your fishmonger. After all, look at all the time you will save, and if you feel like I do, you will hate to kill them.

LOBSTER SALAD

Our most popular summer dish.

1 cooked crayfish (lobster)

lettuce

mayonnaise or tartare sauce or potato salad,
 parsley and orange slices

stuffed olives (optional)

salad ingredients to taste

Place the crayfish on a cutting board, pull tail out and flatten. Take a sharp knife and, starting from the bottom of the tail, cut evenly in two. Alternatively, ask your fishmonger to split the crayfish. Clean inside of head and take out the long "vein" extending to the tail. Some people like the coral of the crayfish in the head section and eat that. If it is very fresh, and bright yellow, why not? Rinse the crayfish carefully for a few minutes only under running water until the head is clean. Place each half on a plate.

Loosen meat from shell, starting from the tail and chopping or cutting the flesh a little. I always do this, because sometimes the flesh is hard to cut in the shell when you are eating it with the salad.

Place a small piece of lettuce in the empty head sections and fill with tartare sauce (see page 56), mayonnaise (see pages 52 and 53), or, if liked, potato salad, fresh, crisp parsley and orange slices. I like to cut stuffed olives in half and place them on the white flesh of the tail, as an extra decoration.

Surround the lobster with cupped lettuce leaves filled with a selection of your own favourites — such as radishes, pineapple, cucumbers, onions, tomatoes, grated carrots and celery.

Serves 1–2

LOBSTER NEWBURG

1 cooked crayfish (lobster), cut in half
¼ cup white wine
½ cup madeira
1 ¼ cups thick cream
1 small can champignons, drained

salt
dash tabasco
yolks of 2 eggs
lemon slices

Remove flesh from crayfish; place shells in oven to heat.

Place wine and madeira in saucepan, heat and simmer for about 3 minutes. Add lobster, heat through.

Add cream, champignons, salt and tabasco, stirring. Cook for a few minutes until all is combined and hot. When ready to serve, stir through egg yolks. Heat—but careful, do not boil.

Fill hot crayfish or lobster shells and serve with plain, boiled, seasoned fluffy rice, sprinkled over with paprika. Garnish with lemon slices, and, of course, all fish dishes must be served on a hot plate.

Serves 2

LOBSTER MORNAY

1 cooked crayfish (lobster)
butter
2 shallots, chopped
1 bay leaf, crushed

½ cup white wine (optional)
2 cups white sauce (see page 61)
grated tasty cheese
breadcrumbs

If you are feeling rather "lush" and extravagant, buy a 1 kg (2 lb) or slightly larger crayfish. Cut in half. Remove the flesh and slice in scallops. Pop the empty shells (the two halves) in a nice hot oven to get really hot.

Sauté (fry) the lobster or crayfish meat in a little butter, with chopped shallots and a crushed bay leaf, and then add a little white wine, if you like. After the wine has evaporated, add your white sauce and reheat.

Have the griller nice and hot, bring out the crayfish shells from the oven, pop your crayfish mixture in, grate some cheese and breadcrumbs on top, and slide under the griller. Brown all over but please be careful and do not burn. Haven't got a griller good enough? Well, try the hot oven, but it's too slow for my liking and doesn't brown well enough. After all, this dish is "a touch of class" and deserves to be the best. I hope you and the family, or your boss, enjoy it.

Serves 2

93

DELICIOUS GRILLED GREEN LOBSTER

Make sure your uncooked lobster is fresh and has been cleaned correctly after being cut in two. If using a frozen crayfish, be sure to defrost naturally.

1 green crayfish (lobster) split in half or
*   two frozen lobster tails*
dash of tabasco
liberal amount of butter
sprinkle paprika

little salt (optional)
lemon juice
hot melted butter
freshly ground black pepper

Chop flesh of crayfish while still in shell. Sprinkle a dash of tabasco over each half. Add generous dabs of butter, both over and under flesh. Sprinkle over paprika, a little salt if liked (not really necessary) and a squeeze of lemon juice.

Thus prepared, place the two halves on a tin plate or griller, and put under a medium griller, basting frequently and turning over the flesh. It should be cooked in 20 minutes.

Serve your Grilled Green Lobsters with a small container of hot, melted butter and, on the table, your pepper grinder for fresh pepper.

I think this dish is very good served with whole potatoes, which have been carefully boiled, strained, split at the top as though making chips but not cut through, and then brushed over with melted butter and put under a hot griller to brown and dry out. In fact, this is a delicious way of doing potatoes with any dish, meat or fish.

Serves 2

HOT, MOUTH-WATERING, BUTTERED LOBSTER

So, you have your own lobster trap, or you are away on a seaside holiday and you are down the wharf when the crayfish fishermen come in, and you have a beautiful, freshly caught crayfish...

See cooking of fresh lobster (page 91), but don't run cooked lobster under cold water. Remove from boiler and split down centre. Have hot clarified butter (see page 60) melted ready, plenty of it, and freshly ground pepper and salt.

Put on a large bib, start off with a knife and fork, finish with our natural tools, our hands, fingers and thumbs, then your little hammer or nut crackers and a steel skewer for the succulent parts of the claws.

If liked, add plenty of lemon wedges. I just like the flavour of the crayfish, the hot butter, pepper and salt.

A great meal will be had by all!

INDIAN LOBSTER

1 cooked crayfish (lobster)

3 tablespoons butter

1 clove garlic, crushed

1 brown onion, chopped finely

1 stalk celery, strings removed and
   chopped finely

2 teaspoons curry powder

salt

2 teaspoons sugar

2½ cups milk mixed with 2½ cups fish stock
   or water

2 teaspoons cornflour mixed to a paste
   with a little water

breadcrumbs

Cut the crayfish in half, remove flesh and slice. Place shells in the oven to heat.

In a saucepan, mix 1 tablespoon butter, garlic, onion, celery, curry powder and salt to taste. Stir until onion is tender.

Add sugar, milk and stock, and cornflour paste, and heat, stirring, until mixture boils and thickens slightly.

Add crayfish slices and heat through. Pile the mixture into heated shells, dot with remaining butter, sprinkle with breadcrumbs and brown under the griller.

What to serve with it? Naturally, fluffy rice, lemon slices and chutney if liked. You know by now that eye appeal always does the trick, and it's very handy to have a parsley garden. You can always use a substitute for parsley when it is hard to obtain — try chopped up celery tops.

Serves 2

SPRING LOBSTER

This delicious, low-fat recipe for lobster comes from Lucila Maddox, the dietitian at St Luke's Hospital. Lucila was born in Peru and did her training in Buenos Aires.

1 cooked lobster, sliced

2 avocados, sliced

10 artichoke hearts

10 slices pineapple

1 lettuce, shredded

4 slices lemon

walnut halves to garnish (about 20)

Dressing

1 tablespoon sunflower oil

3-4 tablespoons plain non-fat yoghurt
   (or blend of 1 part skim milk to 2 parts
   low-fat ricotta cheese)

juice of 2 lemons

salt and freshly ground pepper to taste

On a large platter, arrange lobster, avocado, artichoke hearts and pineapple slices.

Add a border of shredded lettuce and place lemon slices around the plate. Spread with walnut halves and pour over the dressing.

Serves 10 as an entree or buffet dish

LOBSTER IN ASPIC

2½ cups aspic jelly (see below)

flesh from 2 kg (4 lb) crayfish, cut into neat pieces

3 hard-boiled eggs, sliced

1 carrot, scraped and grated

freshly ground pepper and salt

a few tarragon leaves (easy to grow)

6 capers

1 large lettuce

stoned olives, black or stuffed

oil and vinegar

mayonnaise

1 stalk celery

1 tablespoon gelatine

Pour some aspic in a mould or dish to a depth of about 5 mm (½ in), and when it is beginning to set, arrange over it in a pattern the crayfish, hard-boiled egg slices, some of the celery that was cooked in the aspic stock (sliced) and grated carrot.

Add pepper and salt and rest of crayfish and aspic, also tarragon leaves and capers. Place mould in the refrigerator to set. When set, turn out of mould, arrange on a bed of lettuce leaves, garnish with olives.

Beat up olive oil and vinegar with pepper and salt to make a dressing. If liked, when ready to serve, pour dressing over the aspic or serve separately.

Mayonnaise also adds to this dish, with extra lettuce and tomatoes.

Aspic Jelly

To make aspic jelly, I take the shell of the crayfish and any other fish bones I have, put all in a saucepan with seasonings, onion, celery, herbs, salt and water to just cover, and cook for 15 minutes. I then strain it and, depending on how much aspic I want to make, I add gelatine. For this recipe I dissolve 2 teaspoons in 2½ cups of stock.

Serves 4–5

BALMAIN BUGS

I think the flesh of these cute little Balmain bugs, Moreton Bay crabs or whatever you like to call them is really delectable. Though it is much more tender than crayfish meat, the proportion of shell to flesh is much higher, and you may prefer to buy your bugs cooked, when they are in season, from your favourite fish shop rather than spend a lot of time preparing them.

COOKING GREEN BALMAIN BUGS

12 green Balmain bugs

water

½ cup sugar

½ teaspoon dried herbs

If the bugs are alive, prepare for cooking as for lobsters (see page 91). Put enough water in a saucepan to cover the bugs. Add sugar and herbs. Bring water to the boil, add the bugs and cook for 10 minutes.

Remove bugs from boiling water and plunge into cold water to stop the cooking process. They are delicious eaten freshly cooked with lemon, vinegar and your favourite sauce.

NOTE: Balmain bugs have a strong iodine taste at times. You can eliminate this by removing the heads before cooking, if you wish. I generally keep the water from the seafoods I cook for stock, but the water in which Balmain bugs have been cooked has a very strong flavour, so I discard it.

Serves 4

BALMAIN BUGS AND SEAFOOD SUPREME

This dish is a "special" in our family whenever Balmain bugs are available.

8 green Balmain bugs

500 g (1 lb) filleted skinned fish, boned and cut into small pieces

500 g (1 lb) green (uncooked) prawns, shelled

125 g (4 oz) butter

1 large brown onion, chopped finely

2 sticks celery, strings removed and chopped finely

freshly ground pepper

salt

pinch of basil

2 drops tabasco sauce

1 large clove garlic, crushed

1 green or red capsicum (pepper), finely chopped

½ bottle sauterne

1 teaspoon sugar

Prepare the uncooked bugs by splitting in two; clean out debris from the head.

In a large, heavy pan, melt butter, then add onions, celery, salt and pepper, basil, tabasco, garlic and capsicum; cook slowly for 15 minutes. Add fish, bugs and prawns and cook carefully for a further 10 minutes.

Add sauterne and sugar, stir and bring to boil again for 5 minutes.

Serve in coupe plates with hot garlic bread or toast topped with melted cheddar cheese and sprinkled with paprika.

Serves 4

DELICIOUS SATE PRAWNS *(PAGE 198)*

EVER-POPULAR OYSTERS KILPATRICK *(OPPOSITE)*

Oysters

Oysters the Natural Way

Our favourite way — and I've just had some for lunch!

Allow from 6 to 12 oysters per person, if you are using them for an entree. If the oysters have not been opened, open them and see that the shells are cleaned and that no pieces of shell are penetrating the oysters.

Wash carefully, but please do not wash and wash the oysters under a running tap. Retain as much of the oyster's natural juice as you can. If you have bought the oysters already opened, they will probably be OK, and won't need washing. Do not leave open oysters uncovered in the refrigerator, as this tends to dry them out, and a dry film forms over the oyster flesh. Cover oysters with wet greaseproof paper if you are not intending to use them for a while. Be careful not to make the oysters too cold. The flavour is gone if you do.

Serve on special oyster plates (these have a recess or fixed cup in the centre for sauce) or on ordinary dinner plates with small containers to hold sauces, etc. in the centre. Vinegar, horseradish sauce, tartare sauce (see page 56), cocktail sauce (see page 57) are just a few of the many sauces you can use. Serve the oysters with lemon wedges, freshly ground pepper and salt, and thin brown bread and butter.

Oysters Kilpatrick

24 oysters on the shell
1 teaspoon worcestershire sauce
1 cup cream

pepper and salt
250 g (½ lb) bacon rashers, chopped finely
fine breadcrumbs

Remove oysters from shells and put aside. Put shells on a baking sheet and heat in a moderate oven. Mix worcestershire sauce and cream. When shells are hot, return oysters to shells. Use tongs to handle the shells, as they get very hot. Add a little of the cream mixture to each shell; sprinkle with pepper and salt.

Top each oyster with chopped bacon and fine breadcrumbs. Place baking sheet under a hot griller and grill until bacon is crisp but not burnt and oysters are warmed through.

Oysters Kilpatrick are very tasty served with a bowl of hot pureed spinach and thin slices of buttered brown or rye bread.

Serves 2–4 as an entree

FRIED OYSTERS

So delicious I think you could go on eating them forever and a day.

24 oysters on the shell	*Sao biscuit crumbs, crushed finely*
1 egg	*butter*
2 tablespoons cream	*lemon wedges*
plain flour seasoned with pepper and salt	*parsley*

Remove oysters from shell. Place shells on a large baking dish in oven to heat.

Beat egg and cream together on a large dinner plate.

Coat oysters with seasoned flour, then dip in egg mixture, and lastly coat all over with biscuit crumbs. If liked, you can place these crumbed oysters in the coldest part of the fridge for half an hour to harden.

When ready to cook, melt butter; it burns very easily, so use a low heat, please. Place oysters in and cook slowly until the coating is crisp, about 7 minutes. Drain.

Remove shells from oven (careful of burnt fingers — use tongs). Place oysters in the shells and arrange on plates. Garnish plates with lemon wedges and parsley and serve.

I told you, they are very more-ish.

Serves 4 as an entree, 2 as a main course

OYSTERS ROCKEFELLER

24 oysters on the shell
2 tablespoons butter
1 large clove garlic, crushed
3 stalks crisp celery, strings removed and chopped
finely
½ large red capsicum or 1 small one, chopped finely
freshly ground pepper and salt

250 g (½ lb) bacon, rind removed, chopped
pinch cayenne
1½ cups breadcrumbs or Sao biscuit crumbs,
or more as needed
1 teaspoon worcestershire sauce
2 tablespoons cream

Remove oysters from shells; heat shells under a low griller.

Melt butter in a heavy frying pan, being careful not to let it burn. Add garlic and twist around pan for a few seconds for flavour, then discard. Add celery, red capsicum, freshly ground pepper and salt, and chopped bacon. Cook slowly until all is tender, 10 to 15 minutes. Add a pinch of cayenne.

Mix breadcrumbs with worcestershire sauce and cream. Put aside.

Remove shells from under the hot griller, spoon a little celery, capsicum and bacon mixture into each shell, then place the fresh oyster on top.

Top with bread mixture and grill under medium heat until bread mixture is browned and oysters are just warmed through. If you think the oysters need more breadcrumbs, just sprinkle extra over.

Serves 2–4 as an entree

OYSTER MORNAY SUPERB

Rich, succulent oysters in creamy white sauce. Who could ask for anything more?

2½ cups milk	2 tablespoons plain flour
1 small onion, chopped finely	1 teaspoon mustard
freshly ground pepper	1 tablespoon butter
pinch salt	1 large carrot, scraped and grated firmly
4 drops tabasco	2 tablespoons cream
pinch basil or dill	24 beautiful oysters on the shell
½ teaspoon celery salt	tasty cheese, grated

Put milk to heat in a saucepan, add onion, pepper, salt, tabasco, basil and celery salt. Mix plain flour and mustard to a smooth paste with water.

When milk mixture is very hot, but not boiling, stir in flour and mustard mixture. Add butter, stir until all is combined and thickened. Cook slowly for 15 minutes, stirring occasionally to see that mixture does not stick and burn. When ready, stir in grated carrot; remove from stove and stir in cream.

Remove oysters from shell and add to sauce in saucepan. Return pan to heat to warm through, meanwhile heating shells under a hot griller. When all is ready, fill shells with oysters and sauce, sprinkle with grated cheese and put under the griller again, to brown. Superb!

Serves 2–4 as an entree

DEVILLED OYSTERS

2 tablespoons butter

2 teaspoons curry powder or to taste

1 tablespoon worcestershire sauce

1 teaspoon anchovy sauce

small pinch cayenne

juice of 1 lemon

2 eggs, well beaten

1 cup milk

2 teaspoons cornflour

24 oysters, bottled or on the shell

paprika

lemon wedges

Mix butter, curry powder, worcestershire sauce, anchovy sauce, that tiny pinch of cayenne and lemon juice in a bowl. Add beaten eggs and milk and mix well.

Pour mixture into saucepan. Cook slowly for 10 minutes, stirring, then thicken with cornflour that has been mixed to a smooth paste with a little milk.

When mixture has boiled and thickened, add the oysters. Do not overcook the oysters; just cook for a few minutes to reheat and flavour.

Serve on a bed of fluffy rice, with a sprinkle of paprika and plenty of lemon wedges. If you like your oysters hotter, just increase the quantity of curry powder.

Serves 4 as an entree, 2 as a main course

OYSTERS IN SCALLOP SHELLS

My friend Nola Brown's favourite recipe. She's a keen oyster eater as well as a keen fisherwoman, and in our young days we used to gather our oysters off the rocks around Sydney Harbour. That's giving our ages away — fancy being able to do that nowadays! This is a nice entree dish.

2 cups white sauce (see page 61)	*16–24 oysters*
1 tablespoon worcestershire sauce	*breadcrumbs*
4 tablespoons tomato chutney	*butter*
1 tablespoon cream	*parsley*
salt	*lemon wedges*
½ teaspoon cayenne pepper	*4 scallop shells or ramekins*

Make the white sauce, add the worcestershire sauce, chutney, cream, salt and cayenne.

Put 4 or 6 oysters into each ramekin or scallop shell, then cover with the sauce, sprinkle with breadcrumbs, dot with butter and bake in a hot oven until warmed through and browned on the top.

Garnish with parsley and lemon wedges.

Serves 4 as an entree

JOHN DOYLE'S OYSTERS SUPREME

This is a really superb dish from Doyle's on the Beach at Rainbow Bay, Coolangatta. Oh, what a dish for starters—delicious! And to follow as a main dish, try John's Mild Mustard Prawns (page 83).

2 to 3 dozen oysters
100 g (3 oz) butter
½ cup plain flour
½ cup mayonnaise
½ cup tomato puree
½ cup milk

1 teaspoon curry powder
1 avocado
1 cup crab meat (canned, if fresh not available)
½ cup cream
tasty cheese
paprika

Place oysters (in shells) on an oven dish (such as a scone tray). Preheat oven to moderate.

Melt butter (take care not to let it burn), and add flour to make a roux. Add mayonnaise, tomato puree, milk and curry powder; stir to make a smooth mixture, and cook slowly for 5 minutes. Allow to cool.

Mash avocado and crab meat together; add to cooled mixture. Place mixture carefully on top of oysters, then add cream.

Grate tasty cheese over the top, dust with paprika and bake for 10 minutes.

Serve on hot plates with toasted, fried sippets of bread or thin, crustless brown-bread and butter sandwiches, cut into quarters, or that never-to-be forgotten (day and night hiccups) garlic bread.

MUSSELS

Mussels are delicious, and a really clean shellfish, because all the dirt is on the outside and none penetrates inside. Don't be put off buying them because they are sold in the shell—they are easy to prepare and well worthwhile.

MUSSELS À LA PORTUGUESE

I don't know why we call this dish "Portuguese"—we get the mussels in Sydney. In fact, in my day mussels were exclusive to us Watson's Bay locals. Anyway, it's a smart name and a dish cooked to perfection by my grandson Peter at Doyle's on the Beach at Watson's Bay.

1–1.5 kg (2–3 lb) mussels	*3 teaspoons finely chopped parsley*
4 shallots, chopped finely	*2 fresh thyme sprigs or pinch dried thyme*
1 clove garlic, chopped	*1 or 2 bay leaves*
2 tablespoons olive oil	*½ teaspoon ground black pepper*
3 teaspoons butter	*125 ml (4 oz) fresh cream*
⅔ cup dry white wine	*extra chopped parsley*
⅓ cup water	*lemon quarters*

Wash mussels under running water, and remove all traces of mud, seaweed and barnacles with a brush or knife; remove beards (the rough, furry part around the mussel). If mussel shells are cracked or broken, discard them. If any mussels are slightly open, tap sharply, and if they do not close, discard.

Gently fry shallots and garlic in olive oil and butter until transparent but not coloured. Add wine, water, parsley, thyme, bay leaf, pepper and mussels. Pour cream over the top. Cover pan, bring to the boil and steam over a high heat for about 4 minutes, shaking pan constantly. The shells will open as the mussels cook.

Serve as soon as the shells open. Serve in deep bowls like mixing bowls, garnished with chopped parsley and lemon quarters. Mmmm—delicious.

Don't forget a large spoon to scoop up the juice.

Serves 2–3

SCALLOPS

Scallops are refined, delicate, versatile and more-ish little shellfish — so smart and pretty when they are all cleaned up. There are so many different gourmet dishes that can be made with scallops that once you know a little about them, cooking with them is, to quote my favourite saying, "just a breeze" — like that beautiful nor'-easter that floats across Sydney Harbour on a hot summer's day. Very easy to take (the breeze and the scallops). Scallops can be tough if overcooked, so take care.

BREADED, BUTTERED SCALLOPS

Rich but delicious — great served with crisp bacon and mushrooms.

750 g (1½ lb) scallops

250 g (½ lb) bacon

1 egg

2 tablespoons cream

plain flour, seasoned with salt and pepper

about 2 cups breadcrumbs or Sao biscuit crumbs

125 g (4 oz) butter

lemon slices

parsley sprigs

Place white butcher's paper on your workbench and spread with plain flour. Blend breadcrumbs or roll out biscuit crumbs.

Dry scallops. Cut rind off bacon and cut bacon in small pieces, cutting off as much fat as possible.

Mix egg and cream together on a large dinner plate.

Toss scallops in flour, then in egg mixture and lastly in breadcrumbs.

Melt butter in a large, heavy pan, and when it is hot (do not burn), put in bacon and scallops and cook slowly for 10 minutes.

Serve on hot plates garnished with lemon and parsley.

Serves 4

SCALLOPS AND MUSHROOMS

Mushrooms seem to be at their best at the same time of the year as scallops, and luckily they go very well together.

175 g (6 oz) butter

500 g (1 lb) small mushrooms, halved

½ bunch shallots, chopped

pepper and salt

750 g (1½ lb) scallops

1 small can tomatoes, drained

2 bay leaves

1 teaspoon sugar

pinch basil

1 clove garlic, crushed

2 sticks celery, chopped

4 drops tabasco sauce

breadcrumbs

Melt 125 g (4 oz) butter in pan. Place mushrooms and shallots in pan with some freshly ground pepper and salt, fry gently and put aside until needed.

Dry scallops and fry in remaining butter to which tomatoes have been added. Add bay leaves, sugar, basil, garlic, celery and tabasco. Cook all gently for 10 minutes.

Place mixture in a flat casserole dish, add mushrooms and mix well. Sprinkle with breadcrumbs and place in a warm oven until brown on top.

Serve with hot savoury bread or garlic bread.

Serves 4

SCALLOPS MORNAY

2 large tablespoons butter or margarine

2 tablespoons plain flour

½ teaspoon dried dill

½ teaspoon dried basil

freshly ground pepper

½ teaspoon salt

4 drops tabasco sauce

1 teaspoon worcestershire sauce

3 ¾ cups milk, or half milk and half fish stock

2 bay leaves

sticks crisp celery, strings removed and chopped finely

1 small brown onion, grated

500 g (1 lb) scallops, from your friendly fish shop

1 carrot, peeled and grated

tasty cheese, grated

chopped parsley

paprika

lemon wedges

In a heavy saucepan, melt butter, add flour, stir until butter is absorbed into flour. Add dill, basil, pepper, salt, tabasco and worcestershire sauce, then slowly add milk, stirring all the time until mixture boils and thickens.

Add unbroken bay leaves with celery and onion. Cook, stirring all the time for about 10 minutes, then turn heat very low.

Place scallops in another saucepan, just cover with water, bring to the boil and boil slowly for about 3 minutes.

Strain scallops and place them in the sauce with the grated carrot. Cook, stirring, for about 1 minute.

Pour mixture into individual ramekin bowls or a shallow ovenproof dish. Sprinkle grated cheese over and brown carefully under a hot griller.

Serve as an entree or main course, garnished with finely chopped parsley, a sprinkle of paprika and lemon wedges. Brown or rye bread toasted and buttered while hot is nice on the side.

Serves 4

COQUILLES ST JACQUES

A famous, and delicious, entree dish.

60 g (2 oz) butter

60 g (2 oz) mushrooms, sliced

½ cup dry white wine

250 g (8 oz) scallops

1 cup cream

cayenne pepper

salt and pepper

grated tasty cheese

lemon slices

parsley

Melt butter in a saucepan, add mushrooms and cook 1 minute. Add wine and boil gently until reduced by about half.

Add scallops, simmer for 2 minutes only.

Add cream, a dash of cayenne pepper, and salt and pepper to taste. Mix well and reheat. Do not boil.

Pour mixture into scallop shells or ramekins, top with a little grated cheese and place under a hot griller until melted and slightly browned.

Serve immediately, decorated with lemon and parsley.

Serves 4–6

ABALONE

RUBY BOXALL'S ABALONE STEAKS

Ruby Boxall, wife of Benny Boxall, the Abalone King of Tasmania, often sends us some abalone, all ready prepared for us to fry. We do not sell abalone in the restaurants but enjoy it at home.

Abalone is sold in large quantities to Japan. Cooks in Japan, I have been told, use abalone flesh with other types of shellfish to improve the quality of the fish.

Unfortunately, the abalone in New South Wales are not as tender as those in Tasmanian waters, and the last time I tried to cook a local specimen I had a terrible time. I hammered it, minced it, trying to get it tender, even broke my blender with it, and if I had had a concrete mixer or a steamroller, I probably would have used them both. The result was disastrous, so giving it all away, I buried it in the garden in the strawberry patch. It gave a grand result, strawberries larger than large. My friends wanted to know what fertiliser I was using. I told them "all boloney". At last we come to Ruby's recipe . . .

Select a medium-size live abalone. (Gawd knows where — better find yourself a skindiver!) Remove abalone from shell by cutting muscle off. Then trim off all black parts or skirt that surrounds it. This will reduce the size of the abalone by about a third. With a sharp knife, cut into three steaks. With a wooden mallet or a heavy wooden spoon, flatten gently, carefully tapping the steaks so as not to bruise the meat.

Coat with egg and biscuit crumbs or fine breadcrumbs. Fry in hot oil until brown on both sides. The steaks will take about 12 minutes to cook, and as with all fish, care must be taken not to overcook it.

Have fun!

KRILL

Krill are tiny sea creatures that swim close to the surface of the sea and drift where the tides of the oceans take them. They are one of the first links in the ocean's food chain. (Krill, I was told, is a Greek word meaning to wander.) My son John brought home about 1 kg (2 lb) of them for me to experiment with—they were beautifully fresh and had a strong smell of the sea. They make a delicious filling for bread or pastry cases.

KRILLION PATTIES

2 cups krill

2 tablespoons butter

salt and freshly ground pepper

2 heaped tablespoons flour

2 cups milk

celery

½ red capsicum (pepper)

½ onion

1 small carrot

1 bay leaf

pinch basil

drop tabasco sauce

slices of bread

parsley, chopped

lemon wedges

patty tins (2 dozen)

Wash krill in a fine mesh strainer under a running tap. Pat dry with a tea towel. (Keep separate towels for wiping fish dry.) Melt butter in a saucepan, add salt and pepper and stir in flour until it forms a ball.

Gradually add 1 cup of the milk, stirring constantly to prevent sticking or burning. Add remaining milk, stirring all the time.

Blend vegetables and herbs in a blender and add to sauce with tabasco.

Butter bread slices very thickly, press into patty tins and bake in a hot oven for 15 minutes.

Add krill to sauce and cook slowly for five minutes to allow the sauce to absorb the flavour of the krill.

Fill bread cases with sauce, sprinkle with parsley and paprika, and serve hot with lemon wedges.

Serves 4

Squid (Calamari)

I cannot get used to the name calamari, so I will call it squid. There are so many ways to cook squid that I have read about, but to me they sound rather complicated. So I'm going to leave you all to sort those recipes out and just give you two of our recipes—our son Tim's specialities. Squid is naturally tough to me, but I know it has a flavour all of its own.

Calamari Deluxe

1 kg (2 lb) squid, thoroughly cleaned and skinned
1 cup olive oil
1 large clove garlic, crushed
salt and pepper
½ teaspoon dried mixed dill and basil or oregano

1 cup sauterne
500 g (1 lb) ripe tomatoes or 1 can tomatoes, drained
2 teaspoons chopped parsley
small squares bread fried in olive oil for croutons

Wash squid, pat dry and cut into rings.

Heat oil in a heavy frying pan or saucepan, add garlic and cook for about 2 minutes. Then discard the garlic; otherwise it will mask the real flavour of the squid.

Fry squid in the oil for about 3 minutes or until transparent. Season with salt and pepper (freshly ground for better flavour), add herbs and cook slowly for another 3 minutes.

Add tomatoes, parsley and sauterne, put lid pan on and simmer for a further 4 minutes. Have hot plates ready and serve squid with fried bread croutons.

Serves 4–6

Deep-fried Squid

1 kg (2 lb) squid, thoroughly cleaned and skinned
pepper and salt
plain flour

batter (see page 122)
olive oil for deep-frying
lemon wedges

Wash squid and pat dry. Cut into rings and toss in flour seasoned with salt and pepper.

Dip squid in batter and deep-fry carefully in hot oil for about 3 minutes until golden. Serve hot with bread and lemon wedges.

Serves 4–6

SEAFOOD EXTRAVAGANZAS

DOYLE'S PAELLA

As served at Doyle's on the Beach, Watson's Bay. I am not really giving away trade secrets, as the only secret of seafood cooking is fresh seafood.

50 g (2 oz) squid, cleaned and cut into rings

¼ cup Spanish olive oil

1 tomato, peeled, seeded and chopped

2 tablespoons tomato paste

½ brown onion, chopped

1 clove garlic, finely chopped

2–3 bay leaves

50 g (2 oz) green prawns, shelled

1½ kg (3 lb) green mud crab, cut in 3 pieces

3 or 4 mussels, cleaned

200 g (6 oz) fillets white fish, cut in pieces

¼ cup water

¾ cup dry white wine

½ teaspoon paprika

salt and freshly ground pepper

3 cups cooked rice

saffron or paprika and finely chopped parsley

As large squid can take a long while to cook, I suggest you boil it first for an hour. In a deep serving/cooking saucepan, heat the oil, add tomato, tomato paste, onion, garlic and bay leaves, stir well and add prawns, crab pieces, squid, mussels (see page 106 for preparation of mussels), and fish. Stir all again, then add water, wine, paprika, and salt and pepper and stir. Cook slowly for 10 minutes after the ingredients have come to the boil.

Serve in the pot you cooked it in.

Serve with a dish of hot fluffy rice sprinkled with saffron or lightly dusted with paprika and finely chopped parsley.

NOTE: This dish is good with garlic bread. To make it, take a stick of French bread and split it down the centre, butter heavily and spread with chopped garlic, damp all over with milk and place in a very hot oven. Decrease heat, warm through and serve. For a change, I like to brush the top of the bread with melted butter and sprinkle it with salad herbs.

Serves 2

DOYLE'S FAMOUS PAELLA *(OPPOSITE)*

LOBSTER MORNAY, AT DOYLE'S AT THE QUAY *(PAGE 93)*

SEAFOOD BONANZA

For this delicious recipe, thanks to Dr Lola Power.

1 kg (2 lb) cooked prawns, shelled

750 g (1½ lb) pearl perch fillets, boned and skinned

2 tablespoons butter

1 tablespoon plain flour

1 small white onion, grated

1 teaspoon dry mustard

1 small leaf fresh basil, crushed

1 bay leaf, crumbled

½ teaspoon dill

1 cup milk

1 carton cream

salt

1 teaspoon pounded tinned green peppercorns

1 egg, beaten

1 carrot, grated

1 large stalk celery, chopped

1 small brown onion, roughly chopped

500 g (1 lb) button mushrooms, sliced

dash tabasco, if desired

parmesan cheese

parsley

paprika

Chop prawns, cut fish in small portions.

Melt butter in saucepan, and when hot add flour, stirring until smooth and mixture leaves sides of saucepan. Turn heat down, add grated onion, mustard, basil, bay leaf and dill.

Gradually add milk, stirring all the time until sauce is smooth.

Add cream, still stirring; add salt and pounded green peppercorns. Stir egg in carefully, add grated carrot. Do not allow sauce to boil after egg is added.

In a separate pan cook fish for 5 minutes in a little water to which celery, salt and brown onion have been added. Drain and try not to let fish break up.

Mix prawns and fish gently with sauce and warm through.

Place sliced mushrooms in the bottom of a heated casserole, then carefully spoon in sauce and fish mixture. Test sauce for flavour, adding tabasco, salt, etc. if required. Grate a little parmesan cheese on top, place in a hot oven for a few minutes to brown. Decorate with chopped parsley and a sprinkle of paprika.

Serve immediately with vegetables such as hot asparagus, creamed celery, potatoes chipped and fried in butter, or zucchinis, heated soft bread rolls and a dish of scooped-out lemon pulp as well as lemon wedges.

Serves 6

PEKING FIREPOT

This recipe was given to me by John Singleton, who describes it as a sort of
seafood fondue gone wrong! It's quite a lot of work, but well worth the effort.
John says that the best thing about it all is that if you are really hungry you can
go on for hours, and even when it's finished, the bits and pieces that have fallen
into the stock—the noodles, cabbage, etc.—make a really good soup. And if you
are not hungry, it is easy to look as if you are enjoying it without really eating
anything much!

1 fresh cuttlefish
500 g (1 lb) fillets of firm fish
500 g (1 lb) scallops
500 g (1 lb) green prawns, shelled and cleaned
2 green lobster tails
3 dozen oysters
4 large crab claws
dry white wine
2 cloves garlic
1 dozen leaves won bok (Chinese lettuce)

1 bunch buck choi (Chinese cabbage)
3 dozen fish balls (recipe below)
125 g (4 oz) fine noodles
1 kg (2 lb) fresh bean shoots
2 large carrots, thinly sliced
90–125 g (3–4 oz) zucchinis
8 cups hot cooked brown rice (1 cup per person)
8 lettuce leaves
8 eggs
10 cups fish or chicken stock, heated

Fish Balls

500 g (1 lb) fish fillets
250 g (8 oz) green prawns, shelled and cleaned
1 tablespoon white wine
30 g (1 oz) pork fat
1 egg white, lightly beaten

1 tablespoon cornflour
salt
1 slice ham (optiona)
won ton skins (optional)

Equipment For Serving

1 large or 2 small fondue pots
Chinese soup baskets

chopsticks or fondue forks
variety of sauces—soy, chilli, tartare, etc.

Cut fish and shellfish into bite-size pieces. Marinate fish fillets and scallops separately in a little
white wine and finely chopped garlic. When time to eat, arrange fish and shellfish in individual
serving dishes.

Make the fish balls ahead of time by mincing together fish, prawns, pork fat, ham and
parsley, then pounding until smooth. Season with salt and wine, add cornflour and egg white,
then leave to stand for 1 hour until firm. Form into walnut-sized balls or, alternatively, make
won tons. (Put a little fish mixture in centre of won ton pastry square, wet two edges and fold
over to make triangle, then wet two corners and press tightly together to form ear-shaped won
ton.)

116

Heat stock to boiling point in fondue dish, and add noodles, bean sprouts, won bok, buck choi, fish balls, carrot pieces and zucchinis. Guests take pieces of fish, dip in boiling stock for 1 minute, then into a sauce, in usual fondue fashion, and help themselves to food already in the pot. You can use fondue forks or chopsticks. (Chopsticks are much more fun—and much more messy.) Each person should have a bowlful of rice to catch the drips.

When the bite-size pieces are gone, drop a lettuce leaf cup into the stock, break an egg into it and poach.

Serves 8

TIM DOYLE'S AVOCADO SEAFOOD WITH MACADAMIA NUTS

A big favourite with Tim's customers at the Quay Restaurant, this delicious entree is truly a luxury meal—but there are times when seafoods are more plentiful, and you may even live near the waterfront and be able to catch your own. While this seafood version is one for a special celebration, you can also use firm cooked fish with the bones removed.

Lobster pieces, flesh from Balmain bugs, prawn meat (all cooked) and lightly poached scallops (or substitute boned firm cooked fish)
350 ml (½ pint) French dressing (see page 54)
2 tablespoons honey

2 tablespoons lemon juice
salt and pepper
1 cup chopped macadamia nuts
2 large ripe but firm avocados

Mix together French dressing, warmed honey, lemon juice, and salt and pepper to taste. When well mixed, add chopped nuts.

Remove skin from avocados and chop flesh into bite-size pieces. Combine in a bowl with seafoods and dressing mixture and refrigerate until ready to serve.

Arrange in deep, attractive bowls, decorated with your usual flair. Serve with hot, crusty bread rolls or garlic bread.

Serves 4

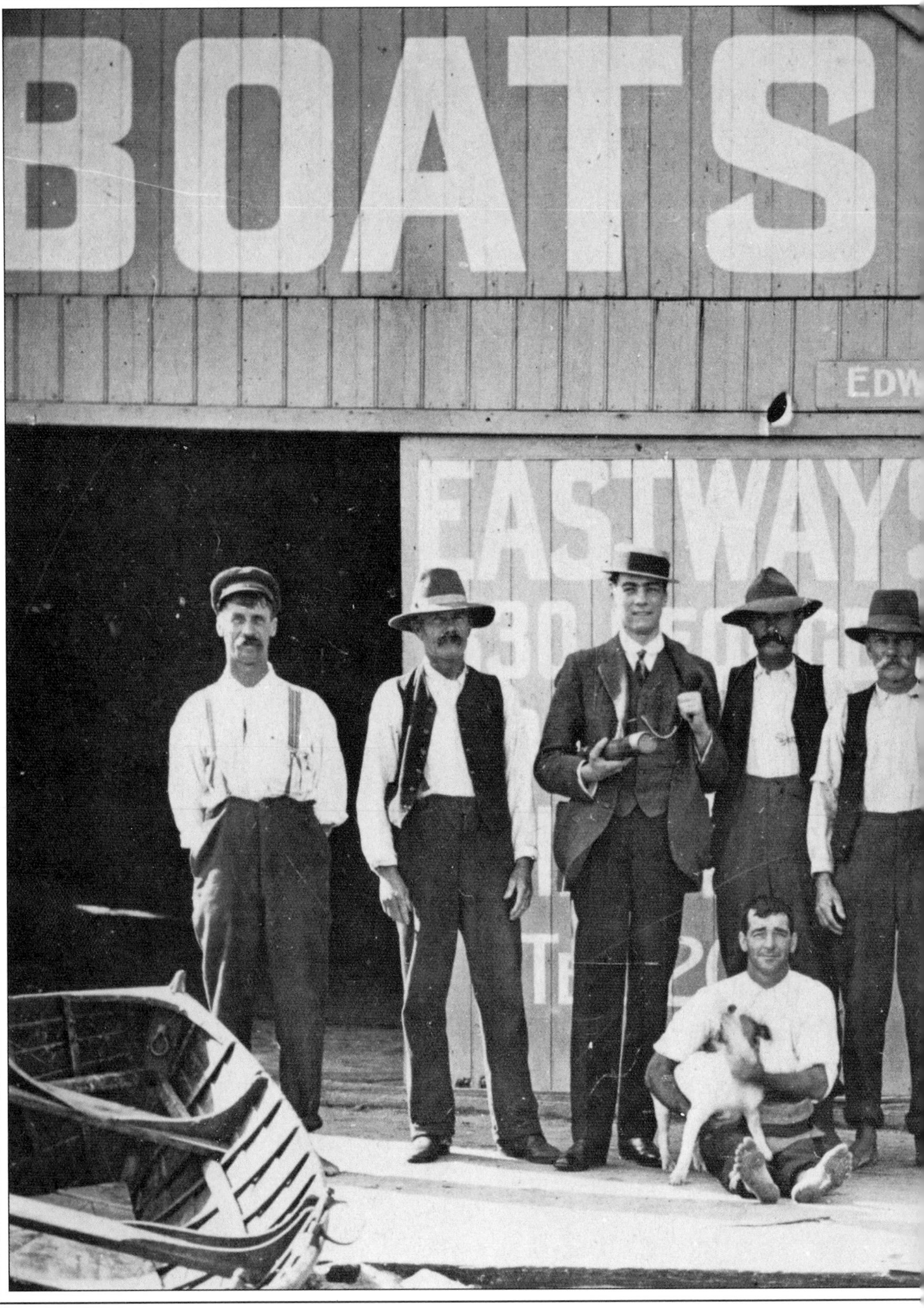
BOATS
EDW
EASTWAYS

OR HIRI

EDWARDS.

FRESH B
PRESER
PRAW
ALWAYS ON H
EASTW

The first recipes in this section are the basics: fish deep-fried, pan-fried, grilled, baked, steamed and poached. The techniques are those used in our restaurants. You can, if you like, simply serve with lemon butter and parsley, or use one of the sauces in the Sauces chapter (page 52) for variety.

Customers sometimes say: "We cook fish at home but cannot get it to taste the same as when we have it at the restaurant. Why?"

Naturally, we buy large fish for the restaurants and fillet them in thicker portions ready for frying or grilling. This also means the bones are easier to take out. With your small family, you do not need fish of this proportion, and you buy small fillets of fish, and generally just flour it, put a little oil in the pan and fry it too quickly. Because the fish is so delicate, it needs only a few minutes in the oil, and when you do not have any covering on it, it dries even more quickly. You get disappointed with your small fillets of fish and start to get frustrated picking bones out of your mouth. Spend a little extra time in selecting fish, and if you happen to have bones in the fish you have, take out as many as you can first. This goes for grilling, too. And remember the following hints:

The fresher the fish, the better the dish.

Please handle your fish with tender loving care. Don't fry or grill it with gay abandon—stay at your stove so you can regulate the heat and therefore have a perfect result. Delicate seafood cooks very quickly.

Remember that small fish or fillets with a lot of bone are best pan-fried, steamed or grilled and served simply, without thick sauces. Fillets or steaks of large fish such as jewfish, snapper and barramundi are good for dishes that contain a lot of sauce, and if fried or grilled should always be served with a sauce as they tend to be dry. You will find plenty of good sauces in the Sauces chapter (page 52).

Before cooking, check that the fish is perfectly cleaned, and remove any odd scales that might have been overlooked. Remove as many bones as you can.

The recipes in this section sometimes specify a particular kind of fish, and at other times give a choice, or do not specify at all. Remember that you can always substitute one kind of fish for another. Just use a similar type of fish to the one in the recipe. If you're not sure of a substitution in season—ask your friendly fishmonger!

The section at the back of the book, Buying and Keeping Fish, will give you information on some of the more common table fish, including their flesh type, availability in different states, and the names by which they are known in different states.

PREVIOUS PAGE: *The Watson's Bay boatshed, 1900. Left to right (excluding the prosperous-looking, boater-hatted salesman): Edward Edwards, the owner; the well-known and highly respected Smith brothers, Alex, Jack and Jim, all net fishermen; and in the bowler hat on the right, Tommy Roames, wearing a bandage that would have been torn from a clean cotton sheet kept for that purpose.*

120

COOKING WITH FISH: BASIC TECHNIQUES

DEEP-FRIED FISH

Fried fish and chips for dinner is a good get-together family meal. Bring out your large serving plates for fish and vegetable dishes to hold the hot chips. Put out plates of cut-up lemons, bread or rolls already buttered, tartare and creamy tomato cocktail sauce (see recipes on pages 56 and 57), even worcestershire sauce (lots of people like this) and vinegar, plus salad, if you like.

Hot plates are essential. Everybody sits down together and serves themselves from the centre plates piled high with fish and chips.

Cool watermelon, rockmelon (canteloupe), honeydew, paw-paw or whatever fruits are in season make the perfect dessert after a fish and chips meal.

The secret of deep-frying is to use plenty of fresh oil. All oil (if any is left) should be discarded after frying fish because of the sediment remaining in the pan. The type of oil to use is a matter of choice. Olive oil is perfect, as the fish is still very tasty and enjoyable when cold. I think it is the only oil that keeps the fish like this. Olive oil is, however, not to everybody's taste, and is not polyunsaturated but mono-unsaturated. Most people use one of the polyunsaturated oils such as safflower or sunflower oil for deep-frying.

For those who have no dietary problems and can eat or fry in animal fats, a delicious frying fat is beef dripping. We do not use it in the restaurants, but as I said in the introduction, I think the best fish and chips I have ever tasted were my mother's — cooked in pure beef dripping. But be warned, you must have it fresh every time you cook your fish, and discard the residue. Obtain your beef dripping from the butcher or make it yourself from beef suet. If you are rendering down the beef suet, please be careful, and do not burn yourself or the suet in the process. Never when deep-frying or pan-frying should you leave your pan with the heat full on. If you are called away, remove it from the stove, and at all times have handy a heavy lid that fits over the pan or saucepan. If you have a fire, do not run outside with the pan, but put the lid on immediately to smother the flame and turn the heat off.

Use a deep, heavy-gauge saucepan — one that you make your jam in or use to cook the winter steamed pudding.

Half-fill your pan with whatever oil you prefer. Heat the oil until very hot but not boiling. Some people say to look for that blue flame that comes from the oil in the pan and put the fish in when it appears. I can honestly say that in all the years I have been cooking fish and observed it cooking in the large deep-fryers, I have never seen that flame. I certainly have the oil very, very hot when I carefully place the fish in, but not boiling. If the oil was boiling the fish would be ruined — cooked on the outside immediately and raw inside, especially thick fish.

Coat your fish with a good batter (see below). Using your tongs, fingers or a slice, place battered fillets of fish in very hot oil and cook for 5 to 10 minutes, depending on the size, until golden brown. Do not try to cook too many fillets at once.

Remove fillets from pan. Drain and, if necessary, place on a serving plate in a very low

121

over it, or cover with foil, and steam over a saucepan.

Serve steamed fish with butter and parsley sauce (basic white sauce with finely chopped parsley (see page 61).

GRILLED FISH

You can just imagine what it must be like grilling fish in a restaurant as busy as ours. It takes a lot of care to grill the fish to a turn, so that it doesn't dry out. There are certain kinds of fish we don't like to grill; flathead, for example, tends to dry out too much — at least I think so. Our method is as follows:

We place the fish in a shallow pan, with a little water and butter. For whole fish, make two shallow cuts on each side.

We then brush the fish with melted butter, pop it under a hot griller, reduce the heat slightly, and baste again as it is cooking. Cooking time depends on the thickness of the fish — 10 to 15 minutes for thick fillets; for whole fish, 10 to 15 minutes each side.

When ready, the fish is placed on a very hot serving plate and hot butter and chopped parsley poured over. Serve a nice sauce with your grilled fish (see page 52) to correct any dryness.

BAKED FISH

I think the size of the fish to be baked makes the difference between a "triumph" and a "might have been".

Start off with a fish of at least 2 kg (4 lb) — even better, 3 kg (6 lb) or larger.

Preheat oven first to hot, about 210°C (400°F). Prepare fish, making sure it is well cleaned and scaled. Leave the head on. Stuff, if you like, with your favourite stuffing (see page 69) or just sprinkle pepper and salt inside the fish.

Grease a baking dish with butter or oil and place fish in. To make fish "stand up" as if it was swimming, put a small bowl or empty tin in its head.

Pepper and salt the fish, rub over with oil, using a brush or your fingers, and cover fish loosely with foil. Decrease oven heat to moderate and bake fish from 40 minutes for a 2 kg (4 lb) fish to 1½ hours for a larger fish.

When the fish is cooked, remove to a hot serving plate and serve with parsley and lemon or pour over hot, creamy oyster sauce (see page 6). Alternatively, allow fish to become cold, then glaze (below) and decorate with vegetables.

Place fish in centre of table and carefully carve by finishing one side and then turning to the other side. It is best if you can cut the fish in squares if it is large. A big serving spoon is a help, to catch the small pieces as they fall. After you have finished, only the fish's frame should be standing there — just like the fish skeleton you see a cat drag along in a cartoon.

Glazing

Whole baked fish looks most attractive glazed and decorated as a centrepiece on a buffet table. We use the following glaze for our functions and have always found it quite satisfactory. It can be used to glaze appetisers, too — prawns or sardines on biscuits, for example, look much more attractive shining with glaze.

The food to be glazed should have been previously cooked and cooled. Cold whole fish is just as delicious as hot. Dissolve 1 teaspoon gelatine in ⅔ cup hot seasoned stock or hot water flavoured with lemon juice and a little sugar to taste. A touch of sherry is a tasty addition, too. Cool. Lightly brush a little solution over the food. For your decoration on your large baked fish, have ready well-drained fruit and vegetables such as capsicum (thinly sliced), carrot flowers, asparagus spears, etc., and make a few flower arrangements or similar on the food. Paint over again with the solution to give a shiny glaze. If you have trouble in making the decorative food adhere, paint each piece of fruit or vegetable with the gelatine solution before applying. Always store your gelatine in an airtight container.

HOW TO PREPARE A REALLY LARGE FISH

(No yarn attached.)

Credit for this section to our good friend and one-time hotel chef George Heydon.

I asked George how he would prepare a "whopper". Here are his instructions, word for word:

"I think I get more pleasure out of cooking a whole big fish and decorating it than preparing any other dish. The biggest fish I have cooked whole was a 60 kg (121 lb) marlin for the Big Game Fishing Association. I wrapped the fish in 15 kg (30 lb) of dough, placed it on a sheet of galvanised iron and cooked it in a baker's oven. Decorated, it looked super, and it ate pretty well, too.

"Of course, most of the fish I have cooked whole are much smaller, and snapper of about 9 kg (18 lb), or a jewfish (mulloway) about 15 kg (30 lb), are the two that really catch the eye. In a commercial oven, that's about as big as you can go, and even then you have to curl the tail around to make it fit.

"To cook a large fish whole, stand the fish on its belly in a baking dish, with an inverted basin or bowl between the gills. It should stand upright without falling over. With string, tie the tail and pull towards the head to curl the fish around. When the tail is curled around enough, secure the string in the fish's mouth. Tie another piece of string to the dorsal fin and pull it upright, tie in the mouth.

"Rub a little oil over the fish, and add about 2 cups of water to the baking dish. Place a piece of foil loosely over the top of the fish, so that as the water turns to steam it comes in contact with the foil, and keeps the fish moist. The fish will never dry out as long as there is water in the baking dish.

Cook in a moderate oven. Cooking time can only be ascertained by pushing a skewer into the thickest part of the fish, noting the resistance of the flesh and the colour of the fluid that comes out of the skewer hole. I would, as a rough guess, leave the 15 kg (30 lb) jewfish for about 2 hours and then start checking. A 2.5 kg (5 lb) fish should be checked after 1 hour.

"When the fish is cooked, transfer it to a serving platter. Remove string. Some fish look best skinned after cooking. You may cover the fish with a sauce of your choice or even mayonnaise that has been heated and had a little gelatine added to it to make it stick. Garnish attractively with parsley, watercress, lemon slices etc.

"If you like, let the fish get cold and glaze it (see page 124), decorating with raw vegetables and other garnishes. Have fun!"

CURING FISH

fish, cleaned, washed and scaled

common salt

30 g (1 oz) sea-salt

15 g (½ oz) saltpetre

15 g (½ oz) brown sugar

If the fish is large, cut it down the back. Rub inside and out with common salt and let it hang in a cool place for 24 hours.

Mix together sea-salt, saltpetre and brown sugar, and rub the fish well with this mixture.

Place fish in a large dish. Cover lightly but completely with common salt and allow it to remain undisturbed for 48 hours. Turn the fish over, cover it with fresh salt, and let it remain for 24 hours longer.

Drain and dry the fish well, stretching it on sticks, and keep it in a dry, cool place.

NOTE: When keeping fish for a long time, it is necessary to soak it well before cooking.

SMOKED FISH

I must give my thanks for this recipe to my pal of our young days, the late
Ray Thomas, one of a family of six sons born in Watson's Bay.
There are several kinds of fish that smoke well, but tailor, mullet and luderick
(blackfish) are about the best to smoke.

How to Make a Smokebox

Take two standard tea chests, remove the end of one and both ends of the other.

Stand the one with the end on top of the one without ends, making the attached end the top of the box. Then fasten chests together, using the removed ends to "patch" the joins. When this has been done, open one side of both chests to make the door to the smokebox.

Drill eight 3 mm (about 1/8 in) holes 5 cm (about 2 in) apart in the side of the box, about 5 cm (about 2 in) from the top. Do this to both sides of the box, with 30 cm (about 12 in) between rows of holes. Make wire skewers (No. 8 wire preferably) 45 cm (about 18 in) long to fit across the inside of the box. Stand the box on a flat surface.

*fish, gutted, washed and cleaned, minus backbone
  and head*

1 kg (2 lb) cooking salt

½ kg (1 lb) brown sugar

water

Split the fish down the back. Mix salt and sugar well. Rub this mixture into the flesh of fish, then place them in a clean container. (A plastic dustbin makes a good container.)

Add enough fresh water to cover fish and let stand for 1½ hours. Remove from brine and hang fish in the smokebox and let drip-dry.

When the fish feel sticky to touch, they are ready for smoking.

Use clean sawdust; place in bottom of the smokebox and light. Keep smoke on fish for 9 hours, then remove from box.

Keep your smoked fish in a cool place for future use.

DRIED FISH

My grandson Jim is a very keen fisherman. I don't want to brag, but he has the "touch" of holding a fishing line! Jim brought me up some of his dried tuna and mackerel to taste the other day. I thought it was deliciously "chewy", with a real sea flavour, and could be used amongst savoury hors d'oeuvres. Here is the simple way to do it:

tuna or mackerel
coarse salt

Take the backbone out of the fish. Salt fish heavily and leave for 24 hours.

Wash off salt and leave in the sun for 2 days. Cover with a muslin food umbrella if you like, just in case one of our notorious flies lands on it.

Serve with buttered toast fingers or biscuits.

SALTED FISH

This method of salting fish is particularly suited to herrings, mackerel and other small varieties.

fish, fresh, unwashed, scaled and cleaned
brine (water with enough common salt
added to float an egg)
salt

Completely cover fish in strong brine and allow to stand for 18 hours.

Drain well; place fish in layers in an earthenware vessel, covering each layer thickly with salt. Cover completely to exclude the air, and store in a cool, dry place.

GOOD OLD-FASHIONED FISH RECIPES

Here are some great old recipes for fish stews, fish pies, barbecued fish, fish in aspic, fish rissoles, and a lovely whiting mould. They are all favourites of mine, cooked by my grandmother, my mother or my old friends at Watson's Bay for many years and now enjoyed regularly by our family at home. They're hard to beat!

HANNAH NEWTON'S FISH STEW

Grandma Newton used to tell us that at times she had to do the best she could for dinner with Grandfather's catch of the day. I know that backwards, and I often think it's a wonder my sister and I can look a fish in the eye. But any day you walk into my home you will find fish in the fridge! Here's Hannah's makeshift meal. Use one, all or some of the seafood I mention.

black or silver bream, cleaned, scaled and washed

leatherjackets, cleaned, skinned and washed

sand flathead, cleaned, scaled and washed

blue swimmer crabs, prepared for cooking

dripping or oil for frying

1 teaspoon salt

2 kg (4 lb) potatoes, peeled and chopped finely

3 large onions, chopped

thyme

Put fish into a large pot, boiler or fish kettle.

In a large pan, fry onions, stirring all the time. Add salt. Add potatoes and fill the pan with water. Boil for a few minutes, then pour over the fish. Add more water if necessary to cover all the fish. Add thyme and simmer for about 20 minutes.

Serve with Hannah Newton's homemade bread (see opposite). Do not overcook the fish, and take care when eating fish with small bones!

Serves 6

HANNAH NEWTON'S HOMEMADE BREAD

This is the bread we used to eat with Hannah Newton's Stew (opposite). Nice to
eat warm, with plenty of fresh, creamy butter!

500 g (1 lb) self-raising flour　　　　　　*1 tablespoon butter or margarine*
1 teaspoon salt　　　　　　　　　　　　*½ teaspoon bicarbonate of soda*
1 cup milk　　　　　　　　　　　　　　*1 tablespoon brown vinegar*

Sift flour and salt together in a large basin. Make a well in the middle, pour milk in and mix
into a light dough. Dissolve the butter in the soda and vinegar, and mix in with the dough.

　　Turn dough onto a lightly floured board and knead into a damper shape. Place on a greased
baking tray and bake in a hot oven for half an hour or until nicely browned.

YUM YUM SAVOURY FISH DISH

2 large onions, sliced in rings　　　　　　*pinch basil*
90 g (3 oz) butter　　　　　　　　　　　*freshly ground pepper*
6 cloves　　　　　　　　　　　　　　　*salt*
1 piece preserved ginger or few slices green ginger　　　*6 slices thick fish (gemfish, jewfish, teraglin, etc.)*

Put onions in a large saucepan with butter; add ginger, cloves and other seasonings, and cook
gently until onions are soft. Be careful not to burn them.

　　When cooked, place the fish in the saucepan, cover with water and cook carefully for 15
minutes, making sure the lid of the saucepan is tightly closed.

　　With this dish, a sweet and sour sauce can be served (see page 63), if you like. Crisp baked
potatoes are a good accompaniment, too.

Serves 6

FISH HEAD STEW

Ask your friendly fishmonger in advance about the heads and he will be able to keep some for you.

1 large head of any fish (jewfish, cod, snapper, kingfish, etc.), scaled

salt and pepper

3 tablespoons vinegar

butter

1 onion, chopped

500 g (1 lb) mushrooms, chopped

2 large tomatoes, chopped

2 sticks celery, chopped

1 tablespoon cornflour

1 tablespoon worcestershire sauce

2 dashes tabasco sauce

curry powder (optional)

Boil the fish head in sufficient water to cover it. Add salt, pepper and vinegar. After it has come to the boil, simmer slowly for 20 minutes. Be careful not to break its shape.

Fry the vegetables carefully in a little butter. Keep stirring them so that they do not burn.

Pour water off the fish head and add the vegetables. Make a paste of the cornflour with a little water, and the worcestershire and tabasco sauces. Stir in curry, if desired. Add to the fish and vegetables and cook gently for 10 minutes or so (depending on the size of the fish head).

Place in a baking dish or large casserole and serve with the head in a "swimming" position, the vegetables surrounding it.

Serve this dish with fresh fried chips. You'll need fingers, thumbs and a spoon!

JIM SMITH'S CURRIED FISH

What a healthy, much loved character was Jim Smith of Watson's Bay. He lived a long, long life and existed mainly on his own catches of fish. Many a time I've had this, his dish, which he made with whatever he caught that day. Flathead was one of his favourites, as was rock cod. This dish is extra good nowadays with gemfish.

60 g (2 oz) butter or dripping

1 kg (2 lb) flathead (or cod, gemfish, etc.), washed, dried, skinned and boned, and cut into chunks about 4 cm (1½ in) square

1 medium brown onion, sliced

2 teaspoons curry powder

1 tablespoon plain flour

2 cups fish stock (see page 41)

1 tablespoon lemon juice

cayenne pepper

salt and pepper

Melt the butter in a saucepan and fry fish lightly for a few minutes. Take out and set aside.

Put onion, curry powder and flour in the pan. Make sure there is enough butter to fry and cook slowly for 15 minutes. Do not let the onion get too brown.

Add stock, stir until it boils and then simmer for 20 minutes. Add lemon juice and a sprinkle of cayenne pepper.

Add fish very, very slowly. On a low flame, cook for 30 minutes so that the fish absorbs the curry flavour. Make sure you put a tight-fitting lid over the saucepan. Stir occasionally so the fish does not stick to the bottom and burn.

Serve with some old-fashioned chutney, boiled rice, and lemon wedges.

NOTE: Be careful of small bones in the fish.

Serves 4 or 5

131

THE GREAT AUSTRALIAN FISH PIE

This will rival the meat pie! Delicious!

Pastry

300 g (10 oz) butter or margarine

2 cups plain flour

2 cups self-raising flour

2 eggs

½ cup cold water

½ teaspoon salt

extra plain flour for rolling out

Fish for Filling

1.5 kg (3 lb) thick fish, filleted, boned, cut up

fish bones (optional)

1 brown onion, cut up

2 sticks celery, including tops, cut up

4 bay leaves

1 teaspoon basil

1 teaspoon dill

1 teaspoon salt

water

Filling Mixture

2 tablespoons butter

½ cup plain flour

fish stock (see page 41)

fish, prepared as directed, flaked

3 sticks celery, strings removed and chopped finely

½ small can anchovies, chopped

1 teaspoon worcestershire sauce

tabasco sauce to taste

dill

basil

½ teaspoon nutmeg

parsley

paprika

To make pastry, rub butter or margarine in flour and salt until it resembles fine breadcrumbs. (If you have a blender or a food processor, it's a breeze!)

Beat eggs in the water for a couple of seconds until mixed. Add water and eggs to flour mixture and stir in till you have a nice wet dough. If the dough is too hard, add some more water. You will soon get the feel of it. If you think, "I will have to put more flour as I roll it out and it will not be so 'short'," don't worry. After you have rolled it out you can spread some more margarine or butter over it before you fold up and roll again.

Roll out pastry to fit the tins you are using. Make the pastry thin. Grease tins, place pastry in; prick bottom of pastry and place some greaseproof paper in centre. Put some dried beans or something like that on top of paper to stop pastry from rising in the centre.

Cook in a medium oven until lightly browned. Take out and discard paper and beans.

To prepare the fish for the filling mixture, place fish and, if you have them, the fish bones as well in a large boiler. Cover with water. Add vegetables and the seasonings, including salt.

Bring to the boil and simmer for 15 minutes. When cooked, strain everything through a fine strainer or cloth and reserve stock.

When cool enough to handle, separate fish from vegetables and take away all bones. Set aside until ready for use in filling mixture.

For the filling mixture, place butter in saucepan and melt. Add flour and with a wooden spoon stir until all flour is absorbed. Slowly stir in the stock and gradually add more stock to a thick consistency. You will not use all the stock; put it aside for use in other recipes.

Add flaked fish, celery, anchovies and seasonings, including salt, if needed. Cook for only 5 minutes. If you think the mixture is a bit thin, make up some white sauce (milk, butter and plain flour or cornflour), and when cooked, add this to the mixture. Add in parsley.

Place the mixture in the cooked pie shells, sprinkle with paprika. Alternatively, put a glaze on top of the pie before warming through. Beat two eggs with about 6 tablespoons cream and a pinch of cayenne pepper and brush over each pie. Place back in oven and warm through for about 10 minutes.

Serve very hot with side vegetables.

NOTE: Anchovies are quite salty, so be careful when adding salt to this dish.

Makes 4 pies, size of pizza or pavlova plate. I always make a number and freeze a couple for later use.

TASTY FISH CASSEROLE

1 kg (2 lb) fish fillets
butter
2 brown onions, chopped
1 kg (2 lb) potatoes, parboiled and sliced

1 bay leaf, crushed
freshly ground pepper
salt

Steam fish for 10 minutes in enough water to cover. Retain stock.

Fry onions in butter until tender, but do not burn. Place fillets of cooked fish and sliced potatoes alternately in casserole dish, ending with potatoes on top. Cover with stock from fish, to which bay leaf, pepper and salt have been added.

Place, uncovered, in a hot oven. Decrease heat to moderate and cook until contents are heated through (about 20 minutes).

Serves 4 or 5

SAVOURY FISH PIE

You'll need a top and a bottom for this pie! See The Great Australian Fish Pie for the basic pastry mixture.

750 g (1 ½ lb) fish, boned and filleted

60 g (2 oz) butter

1 brown onion, chopped

garlic (optional)

2 sticks celery, chopped finely

1 capsicum, chopped

4 medium tomatoes or 1 can tomatoes, drained (reserve juice)

2 bay leaves, crushed

½ teaspoon basil

½ teaspoon dill

1 teaspoon sugar

freshly ground pepper

salt

chopped parsley

pastry for pie case and top (see page 132)

1 cup wine or water or juice of canned tomatoes

milk or cream

Poach fish gently in water and salt for 10 minutes.

Melt butter in pan and fry onions without browning. If wanted for flavour, rub a clove of garlic around the pan and then discard.

Add celery, capsicum, tomatoes, bay leaves, basil, dill, sugar, pepper and salt. Fry everything together for 15 minutes. Add wine or other liquids and cook for a further 5 minutes.

Add flaked fish and parsley. Stir and warm through. Turn heat off.

Roll out pastry for top and bottom of pie, as thin as possible. Line a pie plate with one piece of pastry.

Place fish mixture in pie case. Cover with pastry and brush with milk or cream. Bake in a warm oven until top is brown.

Serve this pie with creamy mashed potatoes.

NOTE: You can use this recipe for curried fish pies and all kinds of combinations of seafoods. The main thing to remember is to be sure you have boned the fish well before putting it into the pie shell.

Serves 3–4

FISH AND CHEESE PIE

pastry shell (see page 132)

500 g (1 lb) fish fillets, steamed and boned

½ can anchovies, chopped

2 sticks celery, chopped finely

2 small, firm tomatoes, sliced

½ onion, grated

1 cup white sauce (see page 41)

pinch paprika

pinch nutmeg

pinch basil

pinch dill

2 eggs

½ cup cream

3 drops tabasco sauce

½ cup parmesan cheese, grated, or ¾ cup tasty cheddar cheese, grated

parsley to garnish

Cool fish, place small pieces on the pastry shell. Add anchovies and scatter around. Arrange tomatoes, celery and onion over.

Mix paprika, nutmeg, basil, dill into the white sauce, add sauce to the fish in pastry shell, spoon by spoon.

Beat up eggs in cream with tabasco and then gently pour all over the mixture. Put pie back into warm oven and cook slowly for 15 minutes.

Remove pie from oven; spread cheese on top and place under a hot grill to brown. Be careful of burning if you are using the parmesan and not cheddar.

FISH CAKES

800 g red curry paste (easily obtainable at most big supermarkets)

2 kg minced red fish (or any variety of fish)

6 eggs, beaten

pinch salt

¼ cup sugar (or to taste)

½ cup honey

ground pepper to taste

chopped parsley

3 teaspoons anchovy sauce

chopped snake beans or French beans

oil for frying

Mix all ingredients together. Shape like hamburgers and dust with flour.

Cook in a pan or small deep fryer with a lot of (preferably olive) oil.

Serve with sauce of your choice.

Serves 6

135

EVA NEWTON'S FISH PIE

A specialty of my mother, who, I should say, was a cook with no Cordon Bleu diploma; but she didn't need one. Mum loved to cook and I do too, but I think Mum had it over me with lots of dishes. This was one of her masterpieces. Delicious!

1 kg (2 lb) thick fish (cod, gemfish, snapper, jewfish, etc.)

1 dozen scallops

6 large green prawns, peeled

1 dozen oysters (fresh or bottled)

1 teaspoon salt

freshly ground pepper

bay leaf

pinch basil

nutmeg

1 cup melted butter or clarified butter (see page 60)

500 g (1 lb) shortcrust pastry or mashed potatoes

grated cheese

cream

paprika

Cook fish, scallops and prawns in enough water to cover for 8 minutes.

Put oysters in a saucepan, cover with a little water. If fresh, shell and add juice from shells to pan too. Simmer for a few minutes.

Divide the fish into large flakes and place in a dish. Lay the oysters on top, season with salt and pepper, nutmeg and other seasonings. Add the melted or clarified butter and cover with shortcrust or with mashed potatoes. Sprinkle cheese on top, wipe over with cream, add a sprinkle of paprika and bake until brown.

Serves 5–6

FLATHEAD PIE

1 dozen oysters (bottled or fresh)
750 g (1½ lb) flathead, boned, steamed and cold
1 cup melted butter or clarified butter (see page 60)
freshly ground pepper

salt
pinch nutmeg
250 g (½ lb) short pastry or mashed potatoes

Simmer oysters for a few minutes in a little water. Divide the fish into large flakes, put half of it into a dish, lay the oysters on top; add melted butter, sprinkle with nutmeg and cover with the rest of the fish.

Cover dish with shortcrust pastry or mashed potatoes.

Bake in a warm oven for 30 minutes.

Serve with vegetable sauce (below), if you like, or plain with vegetables and lemon.

Serves 5-6

VEGETABLE SAUCE FOR FLATHEAD PIE

4 medium, ripe tomatoes, chopped
2 stalks celery, chopped finely
1 onion, chopped finely
1 teaspoon sugar

½ teaspoon basil
1 bay leaf
parsley
lemon wedges

Put all in a saucepan and cook for 10 to 15 minutes. Sprinkle with parsley and lemon wedges.

SOUSED MULLET

A very old-fashioned way of cooking mullet, which will always be remembered among our favourite fish dishes. It can be prepared the day before and left in the fridge until ready for use. An economical dish, it can be served hot or cold. If it were in a tin and imported from overseas, it would be considered a gourmet dish. Here in Australia, because of the abundance of mullet, not enough praise is given to it. You may know this recipe and can improve on it with a few extra seasonings or vegetables — I like it this way.

4 large fillets of mullet
brown vinegar, enough to cover fillets
3 cloves
6 peppercorns
2 bay leaves
½ teaspoon mixed spice

½ teaspoon ginger powder (or I like 2 or 3 pieces preserved ginger, chopped)
salt to taste
2 drops tabasco sauce
2 brown onions, sliced

Clean fish and rub any black parts off the side of fillets. Place fish in casserole dish, large enough to hold fillets easily, and cover with vinegar.

Add seasonings and onions. Cover and place in hot oven. Decrease heat and bake for 15 to 30 minutes, depending on size and thickness of fillets. Serve hot or cold: hot with creamy mashed potatoes and cold with crisp lettuce and dressing — or you may prefer boiled potatoes.

Serves 4–5

FISH ROES WITH MUSHROOM SAUCE

8 fresh soft fish roes
60 g (2 oz) butter
4 button mushrooms, finely sliced
1 shallot, finely chopped
parsley, finely chopped

4 tablespoons thick brown sauce (see below)
1 tablespoon lemon juice
dash anchovy essence
1 cup breadcrumbs, lightly browned in a warm oven or under griller

Brown Sauce

1 tablespoon butter
1 tablespoon plain flour
2 beef cubes

1 cup hot water
pepper and salt

Grease heatproof ramekin dishes or saucers with a little butter. Heat half the butter in a small pan, put in mushrooms, shallot and parsley, sauté lightly, then drain off butter into another pan.

Add the brown sauce, lemon juice and anchovy essence to the mushroom mixture, season to taste, and when hot pour a teaspoonful into each ramekin or saucer.

Reheat the used butter, toss the roes gently in it until lightly browned, then place one in each ramekin and cover with the remainder of the mushroom sauce.

Spread a thin layer of breadcrumbs on top, and dot with butter and bake in a hot oven for 6 or 7 minutes. Serve very hot.

To make the brown sauce, melt the butter in a saucepan, stir in the flour, blend together until flour is lightly browned, gradually add beef cubes dissolved in the hot water, stirring all the time until thickened, add pepper and salt and cook for about 3 minutes.

Serves 8

SEAFOOD IN ASPIC OR FISH BRAWN

A summer treat!

1 kg (2 lb) thick fish fillets (gemfish, jewfish, cod, flathead, etc.), boned and skinned

1 cup water

salt

1 carrot, grated finely

1 onion, chopped finely

2 stalks celery, chopped finely

½ red or green capsicum (pepper), chopped, or radish, chopped

2 bay leaves

½ teaspoon basil

½ teaspoon dill

½ teaspoon salad herbs

3–4 drops tabasco sauce

juice of 1 lemon

½ teaspoon paprika or some saffron

pinch nutmeg

freshly ground pepper

2 heaped teaspoons gelatine

2 hard-boiled eggs, sliced

parsley, chopped finely

Place fish in saucepan, add water, season with salt to taste. Place vegetables and herbs in pan. Bring all to boil, and simmer for 15 minutes. Be careful not to overcook the fish. When cooked, take off stove and cool. Remove fish and vegetables and strain the stock.

Taste; add more salt if needed. Add tabasco and lemon juice. Add paprika or saffron and nutmeg.

Flake fish, place in basin. Make sure there are no bones in mixture. Add vegetables that fish was cooked in. Grind in some pepper; add parsley.

Dissolve gelatine in ½ cup strained hot stock and stir well.

Line another bowl or large mould with the egg slices; place fish mixture in bowl. Pour gelatine mixture carefully over fish. Put plate or lid on top of bowl and put in the fridge until set.

Serve on a bed of crisp lettuce leaves decorated with sliced cucumber, and crisp celery, tomato wedges, potato salad. Your favourite mayonnaise is a nice finishing touch.

Serves 6

FLO'S OLD-FASHIONED RISSOLES

The new generation call them hamburgers, fishburgers, fish patties, fish cakes, etc., etc., but old-fashioned Flo calls them rissoles, and they are very tasty. Here is the recipe.

1 kg (2 lb) thick fish (gemfish, jewfish, kingfish, snapper, etc.), boned and scaled

2 stalks celery, strings removed and chopped

1 small brown onion, chopped

½ red capsicum (pepper), chopped

grated rind and juice of 1 lemon

2 bay leaves

2 drops tabasco sauce

parsley

salt and pepper

500 g (1 lb) potatoes, cooked and mashed

plain flour

1 egg

½ cup milk

Sao biscuit crumbs

olive oil for frying

Place fish in saucepan and add enough water to cover. Add celery, onion, capsicum, lemon rind and juice, bay leaves, tabasco, parsley and salt and pepper; bring to boil gently and boil uncovered 10 minutes.

Cool. Add mashed potatoes and mix.

Form into flat rissoles with your hand and roll in plain flour, then dip in egg and milk. Then roll in biscuit crumbs. You can put these rissoles on a dish and leave covered in the fridge overnight if you want to cook them the next day. Fry in hot olive oil for 10 minutes.

Serve with Vegetable Sauce (see page 61).

Makes 14

THE GREAT AUSTRALIAN BARBECUE

Surprise! Surprise! This time not those T-bones, sausages or chops but beautiful, big, fat fish. Blackfish is delicious, mullet has a taste of its own. Barbecue large thick fillets of kingfish, jewfish or any fish. When it's fresh, it's all delicious. Here is the way we used to cook them at our hotel barbecue, which was outside on the lawn.

2 kg (4 lb) fish fillets or whole fish, cleaned
1 large brown onion, sliced
1 capsicum (pepper), green or red, sliced
freshly ground pepper

salt
½ cup melted butter
tabasco sauce
1 large can tomatoes

Place the fish on very heavily buttered aliminium foil, supported, if you like, in an old baking dish. Put the onion and capsicum over the fish, and add salt and pepper, butter and tabasco sauce to taste. Pour the tomatoes carefully over the top.

Cover with more heavily buttered foil and crimp edges to hold in the liquid from the tomatoes. Place over a low charcoal fire; let cook for about 20 minutes. If fish is large, make a small hole in top layer of foil and continue cooking until the fish is tender. Otherwise, serve immediately.

NOTE: Use whole, unpeeled potatoes wrapped in foil with this fish. Spread over them sour cream mixed with chives or shallots. Really super!

Serves 4

WHITING MOULD WITH PRAWN DRESSING

6 large whiting fillets
2 egg whites
2 tablespoons white sauce (see page 61)

pinch salt and pepper
thick cream
1 chopped hard-boiled egg

Remove the bones and skin the fillets.

Combine the whiting and egg whites in a blender or mortar. Add white sauce and mix well. Pass mixture through a sieve, then add a little thick cream, and salt and pepper to taste. Mix well.

Fill a well-buttered mould, cover with buttered paper and steam gently for about 17 or 18 minutes, or until it is set.

Remove from the mould and serve with fluffy white rice and prawn sauce (see page 66) with a chopped hard-boiled egg added.

Serves 3–4

SEAFOOD OMELETTE

Probably one of the most easily prepared and succulent dishes, and in many cases the cheapest, is the omelette. Suitable for breakfast, luncheon, dinner or even supper.

I never make an omelette until the person is seated at the table, because from the moment they are cooked omelettes start to toughen.

An observation that I have made over the years in the restaurant is that, on receiving their omelette, most people will immediately cut it across the middle, gaze at it for a moment, and then start eating from the end. Why? I know not, but it's a fact! Now, the omelette!

Omelette

3 eggs   *melted butter*

butter   *parsley, chopped finely or fried*

salt and pepper to taste

Suggested Fillings
(You choose your own combinations; choice is unlimited.)

crab   *lobster*

salmon   *fish of all kinds*

oysters

Mix eggs with salt and pepper about 8 times with a fork. Do not beat or whip.

In a black iron or omelette pan, melt a knob of butter until it gives off a nutty smell. Then add your egg mixture, making sure that it covers the pan. Let it cook for about 12 to 15 seconds on good heat, then tilt the pan downwards and push forward with a thin-bladed pallet knife.

Do this several times with a rocking motion until the egg mixture is cooked. If it is a little wet, it does not matter, as the contained heat and filling will finish cooking it.

Hold the pan firmly in your hand and tap your wrist firmly. If the pan is well greased, the omelette will immediately slide forward until it starts to curl down. 'Tis then that you place your filling in. Give it a further few taps to complete the fold and slide it onto a heated plate.

Brush a little melted butter over it and garnish with parsley.

Serve with vegetables of your choice; green minted peas and julienne carrots make an attractive dish. With gourmet foods such as lobster, oysters, etc., the addition of a tablespoon of bechamel or basic white sauce (see pages 61 and 62) to the filling will not spoil the omelette and will make the mixture go much further.

Serves 1 adult

SPECIAL FISH DISHES

Now for some more "sophisticated" recipes—some of my own favourites, like Spanish Mackerel Stuffed with Fruit and Fish Kebabs, and some gathered together "with a little help from my friends". I asked some of the Consuls-General here in Sydney for their favourite fish recipes and recipes typical of their countries, and also invited some well-known personalities to contribute their most delicious dinner party dishes (fish, of course!). Thanks to their kind response, this section has everything from Japanese Teriyaki to Jewish gefillte fish.

I've put recipes that do not call for any particular fish at the beginning of the section, and more specific recipes at the end, arranged alphabetically according to the fish named.

Hope you enjoy these as much as I did when I was testing them!

TERIYAKI

This recipe was kindly supplied by a former Information Officer for the Japanese Consul-General in Sydney, Mr H. Date, with the help of his librarian, Miss K. Hyodo. Thank you very much.

2 fillets kingfish or similar fish, 80–100 g
  (3–4 oz) each (I used gemfish, but you could
  use any large fish fillets such as jewfish,
  pearl perch or flathead)
1 tablespoon soy sauce

1 tablespoon mirin (substitute sake and sugar,
  or sweet sherry, if necessary)
lemon juice or freshly grated horseradish

Marinate whole fillets in soy sauce and mirin for 1 to 2 hours.

Thread each fillet onto two parallel skewers to keep it firm, and grill until cooked. Serve with lemon juice or freshly grated horseradish.

The Japanese cook this dish over an open flame—if you can do this, don't let the fish too near the flame, as it burns easily.

Serves 2

HENRY NEWTON'S BAKED FISH

The size of the fish you bake will depend on the number of people it is required to serve. The following recipe is for 4 or 5 people. Remember to leave the head on the fish.

2 kg (4 lb) whole fresh fish, cleaned and scaled
2 onions, boiled and chopped
1 tablespoon mixed herbs
2 cups breadcrumbs, fresh
salt and freshly ground pepper

1 tablespoon chopped parsley
1 stalk celery, finely chopped
3 tablespoons soft butter
milk

Mix together onions, herbs, breadcrumbs, pepper and salt, parsley and celery. Rub in butter and moisten with milk till you have a firm, wet mixture, but not sloppy. Stuff the fish with this mixture and secure opening with coarse cotton or small skewers. In the opening behind the head, insert an empty tin or small heatproof basin to support the fish in an upright position in baking dish (as if it was swimming).

Carefully arrange fish in oiled baking dish and place in preheated hot oven; decrease heat and cook slowly, basting now and then with a little milk. A 2 kg (4 lb) fish should be cooked in about 45 minutes. The fish is cooked when the flesh tends to come away from the bone.

When cooked, serve immediately. Gently place the whole intact fish on a large, hot oval plate, leaving enough room for you to pour over your favourite sauce. I prefer hot oyster sauce (see page 6). Potatoes baked in their jackets are a nice change, and they can be served in a separate dish with the baked fish as the centrepiece. It makes life easier if guests serve themselves, each one cutting a slice from the side of the fish.

This dish may also be served cold; cook the fish earlier in the day, and when it is cold glaze with a savoury gelatine glaze (see page 124) and decorate with lemon slices, fancy-cut carrots and olives, etc. Accompany with potato salad and hot fresh bread rolls, either garlic or plain.

PACIFIC PLATTER

6–8 large fillets fish

1 tablespoon olive oil

2 tablespoons brown vinegar

1 large clove garlic, crushed

salt and freshly ground pepper

2 bay leaves

1 brown onion, sliced

1 medium can tomatoes, drained (reserve juice)

Sauce

1 brown onion, finely chopped

2 large sticks celery, finely chopped

6 peppercorns

½ teaspoon dried basil, or sprig fresh basil

juice from tinned tomatoes

1 large clove garlic, crushed

Place fillets in baking dish, add oil, vinegar, crushed garlic, salt and pepper, bay leaves and sliced onion. Reserve juice from tomatoes and add drained tomatoes to fish fillets. Put baking dish in hot oven, reduce heat to moderate and cook for 15 to 20 minutes.

Simmer sauce ingredients together in a saucepan for 15 minutes. When fish is cooked, arrange on a platter and pour sauce over.

Alternatively, serve fish with curry sauce (see page 67) or sweet and sour sauce (see page 63), accompanied by sippets of fried bread or garlic bread.

Serves 6

FISH WITH HERBS

This recipe was given to me by Tamie Fraser. It's a simple recipe,
but delicious!

8 fillets fish, each about 100 g (3 oz)

lemon juice

salt

100 g (3 oz) speck, medium fat, finely chopped

2 onions, finely chopped

500 g (1 lb) tomatoes, peeled, seeded and sliced

1 bunch chives

1 bunch dill

1 bunch parsley

½ bunch cress

½ cup sour cream

½ teaspoon tarragon

salt and freshly ground white pepper

2 tablespoons breadcrumbs

Wash and drain the fish, then sprinkle with a little lemon juice and salt.

Place half the speck, onions and sliced tomatoes in an ovenproof dish and lay fish fillets on top.

Chop chives, dill, parsley and cress finely, add to sour cream with tarragon, salt and pepper. Pour mixture over fish fillets. Cover with remaining speck, onions and tomatoes and sprinkle with breadcrumbs.

Cover dish with foil and bake at 180°C (375°F) for 15 minutes.

Serves 4

MONA MITCHELL'S FISH À LA FLORENTINE

4 thick fillets fish
1 cup dry white wine or lemon juice

Topping

1 bunch spinach, cooked   *60 g (2 oz) grated cheese*
1 cup bechamel sauce (see page 62)   *1 cup brown breadcrumbs*
salt and freshly ground pepper

Flatten fish fillets by rolling with a milk bottle or glass rolling pin, and place in a buttered fireproof dish. Moisten with the wine or lemon juice, cover with a layer of greased paper and bake in a moderate oven, 170°C (350°F), for 10 minutes.

While fish is cooking, drain the spinach and chop it finely or rub it through a sieve. Mix with the cup of bechamel sauce and salt and pepper.

Cover fish with spinach and sauce mixture and top with breadcrumbs and grated cheese. Place under moderate heat in griller until breadcrumbs brown and cheese melts.

Serve immediately with baked whole potatoes and sour cream.

Serves 4–5

SHIOYAKI

Another delicious recipe from the Japanese Consulate-General. A simple and unusual dish for a barbecue.

2 small sea bream (morwong)   *lemon juice or soy sauce*
salt   *grated ginger*

Clean and scale fish. Rub inside and out with salt and let stand 30 to 40 minutes.

Thread two large skewers through each fish from mouth to tail, prick all over to prevent sputtering, and grill for 10 minutes each side.

Serve with lemon juice or soy sauce, and grated ginger.

Serves 2

FLO AND ALICE'S SPECIAL FISH DISH

This is a delicious low-fat dish to salve your conscience when you feel guilty about all the wicked things you've eaten, when you should have been worrying about your cholesterol level.
I like to make double the quantity of sauce and put the extra by in the refrigerator to eat later with plain grilled or fried fish which might be a little dry—it's just as nice cold as hot.

vegetable oil

1 large clove garlic, crushed

1 large brown onion, finely chopped

2 tablespoons tomato paste

500 g (1 lb) fresh tomatoes, peeled, seeded and chopped

1 small tin whole tomatoes, drained (reserve juice)

salt and freshly ground pepper

3 bay leaves, finely crushed

2–3 drops tabasco

1 teaspoon fresh basil, finely chopped (or ½ teaspoon dried basil)

1 capsicum, red or green, seeded and chopped

3 stalks celery, finely chopped

1 teaspoon sugar

2 pieces green or preserved ginger, chopped

1 cup fish stock or dry white wine

4 thick fillets fish (gemfish, snapper, jewfish or teraglin), skinned and boned

1 tablespoon dark malt vinegar

parsley

paprika

lemon slices

Into a large, heavy frying pan, pour just enough oil to cover surface. Rub crushed garlic clove well round the pan and discard (or retain and add to sauce later if you want more garlic flavour). Heat oil gently, add onion and sauté until lightly coloured.

Add tomato paste, fresh and tinned tomatoes, bay leaves, salt, pepper, tabasco and basil, then chopped capsicum, celery, sugar and ginger. Cook slowly, stirring, for about 15 minutes, then add juice from tinned tomatoes and fish stock or wine. Cook, stirring, for another 2 to 3 minutes. Add a little more wine at this point if sauce seems too thick.

Place fish fillets carefully in sauce mixture, sprinkle with vinegar, and poach very gently, uncovered, for about 12 minutes (depending on thickness of fish).

Serve immediately on hot plates, pouring cooking sauce over fish and sprinkling with chopped parsley and a little paprika. Garnish with slices of lemon and serve with creamy mashed potatoes. The success of this dish depends on its being served immediately—it's not nearly as nice if left in the oven to keep warm.

Serves 4

CAPSICUMS WITH SEAFOOD FILLING

A plain dish, but one which really brings out the flavours of the seafoods and capsicum. Extra fish may be used if prawns and scallops are not available.

4 large firm capsicums

water

1 brown onion, sliced

2 stalks celery, chopped

1 bay leaf, crushed

salt

Filling

500 g (1 lb) fish fillets, boned (choose one of the firmer types of fish)

12 scallops

6 large prawns, shelled (green or cooked)

60 g (2 oz) butter

½ cup plain flour

2½ cups milk

pinch nutmeg

½ teaspoon dill

½ teaspoon basil

4 drops tabasco

salt and freshly ground pepper

1 egg, beaten

breadcrumbs

butter

paprika

Remove stalks from capsicums, turn upside down and slice off the pointed ends to make lids. Clean out seeds and pith. Stand capsicums in a large saucepan and add water to cover, then add onion, celery, crushed bay leaf and a little salt. Bring to the boil and simmer for 10 minutes; remove from heat and allow to cool in the water. When cool enough to handle, lift out gently, reserving cooking water, and place in a well-greased baking dish. Set aside.

Using the same water that capsicums were cooked in, bring fish, scallops and prawns to the boil and simmer for 6 to 7 minutes. Remove to a bowl, strain stock and reserve.

Melt butter, add flour, stirring, and cook gently for 3 to 4 minutes. Slowly stir in heated milk and bring to a gentle boil, add nutmeg, dill, basil, tabasco and salt and pepper. Lower heat and add beaten egg, stirring constantly—do not allow mixture to boil.

Flake the fish and chop prawns and scallops into a few pieces, add to thickened sauce and check for flavouring. (Be wary of adding too much salt.) Heat through but do not allow to boil.

Spoon fish mixture into capsicums, top with breadcrumbs, dots of butter and a sprinkle of paprika. Brown in a hot oven for a few minutes, replace lids and serve.

Serves 4

GEFILLTE FISH

This recipe was given to me by Vivienne Gershwin, a superb cook
of Jewish food.
For this recipe I think it is important to mince the fish rather than use a food
processor or blender, as the faster methods seem to destroy some of the flavour
of the fish.

Sauce

3 large onions, sliced

2 large carrots, thinly sliced

1 teaspoon salt

½ teaspoon freshly ground white pepper

3 tablespoons sugar or to taste

water (about 4 cups)

Fish Balls

2 kg (4 lb) fish fillets, minced (bream, flathead or
jewfish are all suitable)

3 raw eggs

3 hard-boiled eggs, roughly chopped

3 large white onions, roughly chopped

1 teaspoon salt

½ teaspoon freshly ground pepper

½ cup sugar

½ cup breadcrumbs

In a very large saucepan or broad-based pan, combine sauce ingredients and bring to the boil.
Reduce heat, cover and simmer gently while you prepare fish balls.

Combine minced fish with raw eggs. Mince together hard-boiled eggs, and onions, salt,
sugar and pepper. Mix together with fish and bind with breadcrumbs — you may need a little
more or less than ½ cup. Taste to check that mixture is moderately sweet.

Moisten hands and shape mixture into "balls" about 10 cm long, 5 cm wide and 2 cm thick
(3 in × 1½ in × ¾ in). Lower balls gently into simmering sauce, which should almost cover
them. (You may need to add, very gently, a little boiling water to bring liquid to required level.)

Try to use a pan large enough to fit all the balls in one layer, and don't make more than
two layers. Cover and simmer for 1½ to 2 hours.

Allow fish balls to cool in sauce before removing to serving plate and decorating with carrot
slices from the sauce. Serve sauce separately — it will become jelly-like when refrigerated.

Gefillte fish is served cold as an entree or luncheon dish.

Makes 16–20 fish balls

FISH KEBABS

An irresistible dish suitable either for a barbecue or a formal dinner party.

4 large thick fillets of fish, boned and skinned
12 scallops
500 g (1 lb) prawns (preferably green), shelled

1 large green or red capsicum (pepper)
2 large firm tomatoes
melted butter or oil

Marinade

1 clove garlic, crushed
1 cup red wine
rind and juice of 2 lemons

salt
freshly ground pepper

Cut the fish fillets in finger-length pieces, and mix the marinade. Marinate fish pieces, scallops and prawns for 1½ to 2 hours.

Cut seeded capsicum into long thick pieces and cut tomatoes into wedges.

Thread fish, scallops, prawns, capsicum and tomato on to long skewers and brush with melted butter, margarine or oil.

Barbecue over hot coals or grill under medium heat till tender (about 15 minutes), turning frequently and brushing once with more butter.

Serve with savoury rice and the sauce for dipping, or sweet and sour sauce (see page 63).

Serves 8

STUFFED FISH À LA REMOISE

My thanks for this French recipe to Mrs Monique Dircks-Dilly, wife of the former
Consul-General of France here in Sydney.
Jewfish is excellent cooked this way, or 3 or 4 trout may be substituted.

5 tablespoons butter

3 tablespoons celery, chopped

375 g (12 oz) crabmeat, flaked

salt and pepper

1 cup fine breadcrumbs

¼ cup chopped parsley

1 cup cream

1½ kg (3 lb) whole fish, cleaned and scaled

½ cup champagne

1 tablespoon flour

lemon slices

Melt 4 tablespoons butter; sauté onion and celery until transparent. Add crabmeat, salt, pepper, breadcrumbs, parsley and ¼ cup cream; mix well. Stuff fish with this mixture and close with toothpicks. Place fish in buttered baking dish and pour champagne over. Bake 25 minutes at 170°C (400°F), basting several times during baking.

Place fish on heated serving dish; reduce liquid in baking dish, add remaining ¾ cup cream and roux (see page 67) made of flour and remaining tablespoon of butter. Cook, stirring, for 2 minutes, check for seasoning and strain over fish. Garnish with lemon.

Serves 3–4

BLACKFISH DELIGHT

Fresh blackfish has a rare and beautiful flavour — unique. Once you are accustomed to it, you will want to eat a lot more of this clean, attractive fish. Amateur fishermen have great fun catching blackfish, and attack them with gusto, of course, seeing they caught them. When I was young, my parents had the lease of the Watson's Bay Baths, and at closing time in the evening when the blackfish season was on, the end of the baths would be packed with keen rod fishermen with their little baskets of green weed and wet sugar bags all ready for an evening's relaxing entertainment. A fresh blackfish, cleaned, gutted and scaled, put on the grill or wrapped in foil over the barbecue is hard to beat.

Most people who are used to cooking blackfish grill it or fry it. We sell a lot in our restaurant grilled, served with plenty of lemon and chips. Here is a new way of cooking blackfish, very tasty.

2 large blackfish, filleted, scaled, skinned, with the black adhering to the wing rubbed off
2 cups white sauce (see page 61)
2 teaspoons mushroom sauce
½ teaspoon anchovy essence
1 teaspoon mixed mustard
salt and freshly ground pepper
1 cup breadcrumbs
butter
grated cheese

Separate the flesh from the bones and flake it. To the white sauce add mushroom sauce, anchovy essence, mustard, salt and pepper, and mix. Combine with flaked fish and turn mixture into a well-buttered casserole dish.

Cover with the breadcrumbs, dot with butter and grated cheese, and place dish in a preheated hot oven, turning heat down to moderate at the same time. Bake for 15 to 20 minutes until browned.

Good with potato chips, potato cakes or corn fritters.

P.S. A tip: 1989, and yet keen fishermen, women and children of all ages are still fishing at the end of the Watson's Bay Baths. Hurry and join them—watch the sun go down on Sydney Harbour, relax, and exchange all those fish yarns we like to tell. A superb tonic.

Serves 4

BAKED BARRAMUNDI FILLETS IN CREAMY SAUCE

6 slices barramundi (or cod)	*1 teaspoon anchovy sauce*
3 eggs, hard-boiled	*nutmeg*
2 cups bechamel sauce (see page 62)	*freshly ground pepper*
60 g (2 oz) grated cheese	*dry mustard*
juice and grated rind of 2 lemons	*paprika*

Boil the fish gently for 10 to 15 minutes, depending on the thickness of the fish. When cool, remove the skin, and place fish in a baking dish. Put aside.

To the sieved yolks of the hard-boiled eggs add the bechamel sauce, cheese, lemon juice and rind, anchovy sauce, nutmeg and pepper. Put mixture in saucepan and cook gently, stirring thoroughly until it begins to thicken. Spread it over the fish in the baking dish.

Chop up the whites of the hard-boiled eggs, sprinkle with mustard and a small amount of paprika and spread over fish fillets. Place in preheated moderate oven, decrease heat and warm through.

Mashed creamy potatoes with finely cut cooked celery, onions and parsley make particularly nice accompaniments to this dish.

Serves 6

MURRAY COD

My thanks again to George Heydon. He says that Mr Wynberg, his old tutor chef, always maintained that Murray River cod was the third best fish in the world and that this simple recipe was the best way to serve it.

1 large onion, sliced	*water*
1 large carrot, sliced	*1 kg (2 lb) Murray cod, filleted and trimmed of fat*
1 lemon, sliced	*fried parsley*
1 bay leaf	*butter sauce (see page 60)*
1 blade mace	

Into a large saucepan place vegetables, lemon and herbs and just cover with water. Bring to the boil and simmer for 10 minutes; place fish fillets on top and poach gently for 10 minutes. Drain and serve with fried parsley and a little butter sauce poured over.

Serves 4

BAKED COD

This recipe was given to me by Jill Peacock. It can be cooked in a microwave oven or an ordinary oven.

1 kg fresh cod or haddock
juice of 2 lemons
2 oranges, sliced
2 tomatoes, sliced
2 onions, sliced
250 g (8 oz) mushrooms

½ teaspoon paprika
½ teaspoon thyme
¼ teaspoon freshly ground black pepper
3 tablespoons dry white wine
lemon wedges

NOTE: No salt to be used when cooking in a microwave.

Into a glass baking dish, place the fish which has been freshly washed and patted dry with paper towels. Squeeze lemon juice over fish. Arrange alternate slices of oranges and tomatoes over top of fish, then spread onion rings on top again. Arrange remainder of onions and the mushrooms around the sides of fish.

Sprinkle seasonings over fish and surroundings. Sprinkle wine over all ingredients. Cook 5 to 7 minutes on high setting of microwave, remove from oven and let stand, covered, for 3 minutes. Alternatively, cook in an ordinary moderate oven for about 30 minutes. Serve with fluffy rice and lemon wedges.

Serves 4

SALT CODFISH WITH GARLIC SAUCE

A delicious Greek recipe, given to me by Marika Harris. Try it for dinner,
using Marika's taramasalata (see page 35) as a first course.

1 whole dried salted cod (or any salted fish)

1 cup plain flour, sifted

pinch pepper

1 teaspoon baking powder

1 egg, well beaten

1 teaspoon olive oil

½ cup water

extra plain flour

olive oil for frying

Garlic Sauce

6 cloves garlic

½ teaspoon salt

1 cup mashed potato

2 slices stale white bread

½ cup olive oil

1 tablespoon lemon juice

1 tablespoon vinegar

freshly ground pepper

salt

Soak the codfish in cold water overnight, changing water a few times. Prepare a batter by blending the flour with pepper, baking powder and egg, then olive oil and water. Cut codfish in 10 cm (3 in) square pieces, dry them, roll them in the extra flour, dip them in batter, fry until brown in olive oil. They should be cooked in about 10 minutes.

Remove from pan on to a hot plate or deep dish; keep hot in oven.

To make garlic sauce, pound garlic with salt in a mortar until smooth. Add mashed potato, continuing to pound and stir.

Soak bread in cold water and squeeze dry. Add to potatoes and garlic, pounding and stirring again until smooth.

Gradually add olive oil, lemon juice and vinegar, stirring vigorously until smooth and light. Add salt and pepper to taste.

Spoon garlic sauce over hot fish and serve.

Serves 4–6

SMOKED EEL WITH HORSERADISH CREAM SAUCE

Fascinating eels — this delightful little verse about them appeared in dear late Theo Roughley's book, *Fish and Fisheries of Australia*:

> Strange the formation of the eely race
> That know no sex, yet love the close embrace.
> Their folded lengths they round each other twine,
> Twist amorous knots, and slimy bodies joyn.

After a trip to London once, I couldn't wait to get back to Watson's Bay to make jellied eels, just like the ones I'd enjoyed in Petticoat Lane. The results were disastrous! So, no jellied eels here (I'll leave them to the English), but instead a Tasmanian recipe for smoked eel guaranteed to be delicious. In fact, if you want to be the hostess with the mostest, this simple dish is a "must" for that special party.

Many thanks for this recipe to Susan Ranicar of Tasmanian Smokehouse Pty Ltd, who served it to me at a luncheon at her lovely home in Deloraine (along with platters of the ocean trout the Ranicars farm at Port Arthur — more about that on page 185).

You can buy smoked eel at the usual retail outlets (fish shops and delicatessens), but it's interesting to know how the experts do it. The eels are put into brine first, and then hung whole on rods in an electric kiln to hot-smoke slowly, for about 4 hours. This way they don't dry out. Larger eels are filleted and then smoked on racks in the same way. The Ranicars use only eucalyptus sawdust for the smoking, which gives the eels a distinctive taste. They served portions of their delicious smoked eel with fresh brown Vienna-type bread and butter and the following horseradish cream sauce.

Horseradish Cream Sauce

1 cup fresh cream

about 3 tablespoons horseradish cream (obtainable at most stores)

freshly ground black pepper

fresh dill, chopped

Whip cream, then add the horseradish cream, lots of freshly ground black pepper and, when available, a little chopped fresh dill.

POACHED EEL

1 fresh eel, boned, trimmed and cut into 10 cm
  (3 in) lengths
olive oil
salt
freshly ground pepper

lemon juice
fried parsley
hollandaise (see page 68), tartare (see page 56)
  or your favourite sauce

Rub eel pieces with olive oil, lay on a plate and season with salt, pepper and lemon juice. Let stand for half an hour, then poach gently in boiling water till light in colour. Serve with fried parsley and your favourite sauce.

Serves 6

EEL TARTARE

1 fresh eel, boned, trimmed and poached
flour
salt and pepper
1 egg, beaten with a little milk or cream

breadcrumbs
fried parsley
tartare sauce (see page 56)

Poach eel as described above. Allow to cool, then dip pieces in flour seasoned with salt and pepper, then into beaten egg and breadcrumbs.

Deep-fry to a golden brown or bake in a moderate oven for about 30 minutes with a little melted butter poured over.

Serve hot with fried parsley and tartare sauce.

Serves 6

EEL IN WINE

1 fresh eel, boned, trimmed and cut into 10 cm
   (3 in) lengths

2 cups red wine

1 large lemon, sliced

few sprigs parsley

1 carrot, chopped

125 g (4 oz) mushrooms, sliced

½ teaspoon dried thyme

1 bay leaf

1 blade mace

4 cloves

6–8 peppercorns

cornflour

Marinate eel for an hour or two in the wine with the vegetables and herbs, then poach gently in the marinade with the vegetables and seasonings for about 30 minutes, until tender.

Remove eel from liquid, keep warm.

Thicken liquid with a little cornflour mixed with water and pour over eel.

Serves 6

BAKED FLATHEAD

Although flathead was once **the** fish, with its sweet, tasty, tender white flesh, its popularity has waned in recent years, possibly because of its many fine bones.

There are many varieties of flathead in Australian waters, the tiger and sand flatheads probably being the most choice. Some authorities rank the tiger flathead second only to John Dory for flavour. This recipe and the next are alternatives to serving flathead fried or steamed (see pages 121 and 123).

1 large whole flathead, cleaned and scaled

Stuffing

1 bottle of oysters

fish stock (see page 41)

1 anchovy, boned if possible

1 cup fresh breadcrumbs

1 teaspoon parsley, finely chopped

1 shallot, finely chopped

pinch cayenne pepper

1 egg yolk

extra egg, beaten

extra breadcrumbs

melted butter

Sauce

30 g (1 oz) butter

1 tablespoon plain flour

1½ cups good stock (fish stock, or tin of celery or asparagus soup, or soup cubes)

1 teaspoon made mustard

1 tablespoon lemon juice

1 tablespoon worcestershire sauce

2 cups fresh breadcrumbs

chopped parsley

lemon wedges

Prepare fish.

Cook the oysters in stock to just cover for 3 minutes. Reserve. Cut anchovy in small pieces. Mix breadcrumbs, oysters, anchovy, parsley, shallot and cayenne together, pour in the stock from the oysters and the egg yolk and mix together. This is the stuffing for the fish.

Put stuffing inside the fish and sew up or fasten with small skewers. Glaze fish with beaten egg and sprinkle breadcrumbs over. Place in a baking dish and cook gently for about 1 hour, basting frequently with hot butter. When cooked, keep hot. Do not overcook, as the flathead will dry out very quickly.

To make the sauce, melt the butter, stir in the flour, cook very gently for 3 to 4 minutes, then add the stock and stir till it boils. Simmer for 2 or 3 minutes, then add mustard, lemon juice, worcestershire sauce and the sauce (from the baking dish) in which fish was cooked. At the last minute, stir in the breadcrumbs.

Place the fish on a heated platter, garnish with chopped parsley and lemon wedges.

Serve the sauce in a gravy jug.

Serves 4

161

BAKED FLATHEAD WITH HAM

A delicious recipe from Dr Don Francois, former Director of Fisheries, New South
Wales State Fisheries. He prefers to use dusky flathead for this dish, if
obtainable.
Choose a large flathead, remove the head and discard. Scale and clean but do not
fillet. Cut in steaks; that is, leave the backbone in. This is also a good recipe for
large jewfish and gemfish.

*1 large flathead, cleaned, scaled and cut in thick
   steaks*

melted butter

salt

freshly ground pepper

plain flour

4–6 ham steaks or 250 g (8 oz) bacon

Carefully wipe the fish dry after you have washed it and cut it up. Place the steaks in a baking
dish in which butter has been melted, and season with salt and freshly ground pepper. Sprinkle
flour thickly over fish and bake in a moderate oven for 30 minutes basting frequently and
occasionally sprinkling more flour over.

Cover the partly cooked fish entirely with thick slices of ham steak or bacon. Cook slowly
for a further 30 minutes or less, depending on the size of the fish steaks.

Serve fish on a hot dish with the strained cooking liquor poured over it and the ham or
bacon arranged attractively around the dish.

*NOTE: This is a very tasty dish, which goes beautifully with hot, buttered garlic bread. To the garlic and butter add salad herbs,
chopped shallots, a few carraway seeds and freshly ground pepper. Glaze bread with egg, milk or cream before popping it in the
oven to heat.*

Serves 4–8

WHOLE FRIED FLOUNDER OR SOLE

A simple and delicious recipe!

sole or flounder (1 per person)   *oil or lard for frying*
plain flour   *fried parsley*
salt and freshly ground pepper   *lemon wedges*
1 egg   *butter*
cream or milk

Scrape fish but do not skin. Wash and wipe dry. Leave in tea towel until ready to cook. Lightly dredge the fish with flour seasoned with salt and pepper. Beat egg with a little added cream or milk and either dip fish in or brush mixture over with pastry brush.

Heat oil until hot. (Lard is also good for frying and must be very hot.) Fry fish until light brown (10 minutes should be enough), turning once. Remove carefully and drain on kitchen paper.

Serve on hot plates and garnish with fried parsley and lemon wedges. A small jug of hot melted butter is a nice accompaniment to the fish.

Mashed, creamy potatoes or french fries (chips) are generally served as a side dish.

WHOLE GRILLED FLOUNDER OR SOLE

flounder or sole
butter
½ cup water

Select similar-size fish if possible—one per person. If too large, cut through centre of fish. Do not fillet.

Prepare fish as for frying (see above). Score the fish (make two incisions across centre of fish) and rub some butter on top part, which has rougher skin than the underside.

Preheat griller until hot. Pour water into grilling pan—this will help to keep the fish moist during grilling.

Place fish in pan and put under griller on medium heat. Cook, basting a couple of times with butter.

A medium-sized fish should take 15 to 20 minutes to cook. Be careful not to overcook it, and do not have heat of grill too fierce. Serve as with the fried version, but remember that extra hot butter makes it more enjoyable, as sometimes the flesh of grilled fish is inclined to be slightly firmer.

FLOUNDER FILLETS IN A DRY WHITE WINE SAUCE

I have seen fillets of flounder in freezer compartments in large supermarkets, so I decided to experiment with some—the result was a really delightful dish. If you cannot obtain flounder fillets, you can use any other kind of fish.

1 kg (2 lb) flounder fillets, fresh or frozen

1 teaspoon salt and freshly ground pepper

3 tomatoes, sliced thickly

1 stick crisp celery, chopped

1 small onion, chopped finely

2 tablespoons plain flour

2 tablespoons butter

½ cup milk

1 cup white wine

fresh basil, or about ½ teaspoonful dried

parsley, chopped

lemon wedges

If possible, skin the fillets. Sprinkle both sides with salt and pepper. Place fish in a single layer in a greased baking dish and arrange tomato slices over the fish. Sprinkle with more salt and pepper, celery and onion.

In a saucepan, blend the flour with the butter, add milk gradually and cook until thick and smooth, stirring constantly. Remove saucepan from heat and stir in the wine and basil.

Pour sauce over fish fillets in baking dish and bake in a moderate oven for 30 minutes. Do not overcook. Sprinkle with parsley and serve with lemon wedges and mashed potatoes—on very hot plates, of course.

Serves 4-6

MARINATED GEMFISH

1 kg (2 lb) gemfish or other thick fish

Marinade

2 tablespoons salad oil

2 tablespoons brown vinegar

1 teaspoon finely chopped parsley

1 teaspoon finely chopped shallot or onion

freshly ground pepper (a good sprinkling)

Batter

1 ¾ cups milk

3 tablespoons plain flour

1 egg

½ teaspoon salt

oil for frying

lemon wedges

parsley

Cut gemfish into serving pieces

Mix together marinade ingredients. Pour over fish pieces and marinate for 1 hour, turning the fish after 30 minutes so that both sides absorb the flavour of the marinade.

Make a batter of the milk, flour, egg and salt. Heat oil in a large, heavy frying pan until hot. Dip each piece of fish in batter, drop into hot oil and fry until nicely browned.

Serve on heated plates with plenty of lemon and parsley and, chopped up in your blender, raw vegetables such as celery, carrots, capsicum with a dash of tabasco and a little salt.

Serves 6

BAKED GEMFISH WITH SOUR CREAM

*2½ kg (5 lb) whole gemfish, skinned, or any large
   fish*
butter or margarine
250 g (½ lb) fatty bacon, chopped
1 kg (2 lb) potatoes, sliced

2 tablespoons plain flour
1 tablespoon paprika
salt and freshly ground pepper
1 teaspoon dried basil
300 ml (½ pint) sour cream

Prepare the fish in the usual way for baking (see page 124), making sure it is clean and dry after you have washed it out. Make incisions about 4 cm (1½ in) apart in the upper portion of each side, and fill each one with a knob of butter. Stuff fish with fatty bacon, using small skewers to hold in place.

Line a very well-buttered baking dish with potato slices. Place a cake rack in dish and place fish on rack. Bake in a preheated moderate oven for 5 minutes.

Mix flour and paprika together and sprinkle mixture over fish. Season with salt, pepper and basil. Continue baking fish, basting frequently with sour cream until it is cooked, about 45 minutes altogether. Fish is cooked if flesh flakes easily when tested with a fork.

Serves 6

JIM DOYLE'S GEMFISH DELUXE WITH SPINACH CREAM

This dish is served on the Wharf at Watson's Bay—at the restaurant where you can actually drop a line and catch a fish or, who knows, a mermaid. (Are there any mermen?) The Spinach Cream can be made up to 2 days in advance.

1.5 kg (3 lb) gemfish or jewfish (bones removed)
dry white cooking wine
1 Spanish onion, or substitute
2 small carrots
2 sticks celery, strings removed

some herbs from the garden (e.g. a sprig of parsley, thyme, rosemary—if using dried herbs, use only a pinch of each)
1 bay leaf
salt
freshly ground black pepper

Spinach Cream

½ bunch spinach, stems removed
2 onions or ½ bunch shallots, chopped
200 g (6 oz) butter, softened
2 hard-boiled eggs, chopped
1 dessertspoon olive oil
1 clove garlic, mashed (optional)

parsley
½ teaspoon mustard (ready mixed, or mix with cream)
3 drops tabasco sauce
juice of 1 large lemon or lime (and a little zest, if liked)

Cook spinach leaves with onion or shallots in a small amount of water. Drain well, chop and allow to cool. (This could be done the day before.)

Make butter mixture by placing in a blender, food processor or mouli grinder the softened butter, hard-boiled eggs, olive oil, garlic (if used), mustard and tabasco sauce. Add cooled spinach mixture and blend all together. Then add lemon or lime juice, and pepper and salt to taste. Chill until ready to use.

Cut fish into 4 pieces, place in a deep pan and cover with equal amounts of water and wine. Add sliced onion, finely sliced carrots and celery, herbs, and pepper and salt to taste. Poach fish gently for 20 to 30 minutes according to thickness of fish, basting with cooking fluid from time to time. Do not overcook. (Test with a fork—if fish flakes easily, it is cooked.)

An hour or so before fish is cooked, remove spinach cream from fridge and allow to soften a little.

Lift fish and vegetables out with an egg slice and allow to drain. Keep hot.

Arrange the 4 portions on hot plates, surrounded with vegetables. Cover fish with spinach cream. Serve with small new potatoes, cooked in their skins, and a sprig of dill, fennel or parsley.

NOTE: This spinach cream is delicious served with fillets of ocean trout (see page 185) or any other fish.

Serves 4

167

SMOKED HADDOCK WITH POACHED EGGS

My thanks to Elsa Jacoby for this recipe.

750 g–1 kg (1½–2 lb) smoked haddock　　　*4–8 eggs*
water　　　*1 tablespoon butter or margarine*
enough milk to half-cover fish　　　*parsley*

Allow a generous portion of haddock for each person. Place fish in a deep frying pan, cover with water and bring to the boil. Boil for 1 minute, then carefully strain off the water.

Return pan to slow heat with skin side of fish up and half-cover fish with milk. Allow to boil slowly for about 2 minutes, then carefully turn fish pieces over and continue to cook until fish is almost breaking up. (Cooking time depends on thickness of fish.) Lift carefully on to dinner plates and keep warm in oven.

Into the remaining milk in pan, break 1 or 2 eggs (according to taste) for each person and poach. When firm, remove and gently place eggs on fish.

Add butter to milk, melt quickly and pour a little over each serving.

Garnish with parsley and serve very hot. A side salad goes well with this dish.

Serves 4

SMOKED HADDOCK OR COD WITH A RICH VEGETABLE SAUCE

750 g–1 kg (1½–2 lb) smoked fish
2 tablespoons butter or margarine
½ cup plain flour
1 teaspoon mustard
pinch salt and freshly ground pepper
2¼ cups milk
2 bay leaves
½ teaspoon dill
½ teaspoon basil

4 drops tabasco sauce
2 sticks celery, chopped very finely or blended
1 tablespoon finely chopped parsley
½ red capsicum (pepper), chopped very finely or blended
2 hard-boiled eggs, chopped
paprika
sprigs of parsley
lemon wedges

I used smoked cod for this recipe, and although the fish was nice and fleshy, I thought it was much too bright a colour. So I washed it several times to lighten the colour and remove some of the salt.

Place fish in saucepan, cover with water, bring to boil and boil for a few seconds. Discard water, add fresh water and bring to boil again, this time boiling for 5 minutes. Remove from saucepan, drain and keep warm.

Melt butter over a low heat, taking care not to burn it. Add flour and mix until combined. Add mustard, salt and pepper and slowly add milk, stirring all the time. Add bay leaves and seasonings and keep stirring to prevent sticking.

Stir in celery, chopped parsley and capsicum. Add eggs to warm up. Have fish ready on hot serving plate and pour sauce over. Sprinkle with paprika. Decorate with parsley sprigs and lemon and serve with creamy mashed potatoes.

Serves 4–5

INDONESIAN SPICED FISH

(Ican Bumba Pedas)

My thanks to Mr Rasjidin Rasjid, former Consul-General of Indonesia, for sending me this recipe for one of his favourite fish dishes. The combination of these spices is hot and delicious.

1 kg (2 lb) whole jewfish

salt

2 tablespoons vinegar

mandarin

1 cup oil

3 medium onions, finely chopped

10 cloves garlic, crushed

10 large red chillis, finely chopped

1 teaspoon shrimp paste (terasi/blachan)

2 large tomatoes, sliced, or 3 tablespoons tomato sauce

2 salam leaves (duan salam)

2 slices laos

small piece lemon grass (sereh)

Wash the fish thoroughly. Mix salt, vinegar and mandarin and rub fish with mixture.

Heat ¾ cup of the oil in a large, heavy frying pan and fry the fish on a medium heat until golden-brown. Remove and drain.

Blend the onions, garlic, chillis and shrimp paste, or pound in a mortar. Heat remaining oil in pan and fry onion mixture until brown. Add tomatoes, salt to taste, salam leaves, laos and lemon grass.

Add fish to pan and simmer for a few minutes.

Serve in a tureen.

Serves 4

MOROCCAN FISH

The nurse at our local dentist told me that her mother makes a very special fish
dish twice a week — she gave me this recipe.

6 jewfish fillets

2 onions, sliced

5 tablespoons olive or polyunsaturated oil

1 small can tomato paste

6 olives

1 tablespoon chopped parsley

salt and pepper

Place fish fillets in a heatproof dish on a bed of sliced onions. Add oil and tomato puree and
pour water over until fish is covered.

Add olives, parsley, salt and pepper. Bake in a moderate oven for 45 minutes.

Delicious served with potatoes baked in their jackets, spread with sour cream and chives.

Serves 6

LEATHERJACKET DELIGHT

These beautiful, white-fleshed fish are really a delight to eat — that is, after the
task of cleaning and skinning them is over. They are best cooked whole.

whole leatherjackets

salt

½ teaspoon basil or dill

2 bay leaves

shallots, chopped

celery, chopped

mustard to taste

butter

To make a fish stock, remove tails and heads from fish and place in pan with enough water
to cover, with salt, basil and bay leaves. Cook slowly for 15 minutes. Strain and set aside.

Place the leatherjackets in a well-greased baking dish and sprinkle with shallots and celery.
Add mustard and pour the fish stock over.

Spread butter on each fish and cook in a moderate oven for 20 minutes, basting once or twice.

When cooked, remove fish and place on a hot dish. Pour off liquid into saucepan and boil
rapidly to reduce. Pour over fish and brown under a hot griller.

JOHN DORY CLASSIC

1 whole John Dory or 4 fillets
500 g (1 lb) school prawns (peeled)
2 whiting or redfish fillets
salt
1 bay leaf
freshly ground pepper
1 teaspoon anchovy essence
1 egg

1 tablespoon chablis or sauterne
few drops lemon juice
30 g (1 oz) butter
1 tablespoon plain flour, seasoned with salt
  and pepper
parsley
lemon wedges

If you have whole fish, fillet and retain bones. Remove head. You can make a stock by boiling the bones and head slowly for an hour in enough water to cover, with ½ teaspoon salt and a bay leaf. Incorporate this stock in your sauce or refrigerate for use another day.

Wash fish. John Dory fillets are sometimes large and should be cut down the centre. Remove any bones from smaller fish. Blend prawns and whiting in a blender with anchovy essence and egg or pound them in a basin. Spread the prawn and whiting mixture over the John Dory fillets which have been placed in a buttered baking dish. Season lightly with salt and pepper and moisten with the wine and lemon juice.

Cover fillets with buttered paper or foil, place in a moderate oven and bake for 15 to 20 minutes, according to thickness of fish.

Remove fish to a hot serving plate, taking care not to break fillets.

Melt butter in a small saucepan, stir in flour, salt and pepper to make a roux paste. Stir the roux into the baking dish. Bring to boil on top of stove and pour over fillets. Garnish with parsley and lemon wedges.

Saratoga chips (very thinly sliced potato), fried very crisp in olive oil, are an excellent accompaniment.

Serves 4–5

NANBAN ZUKE

Another delicious Japanese fish recipe, by courtesy of a former Information
Officer for the Japanese Consulate-General, Mr H. Date.

Marinade

2 tablespoons soy sauce

2 tablespoons sake (or substitute sherry)

*mackerel fillets (or substitute gemfish or jewfish),
cut into bite-size pieces*

cornflour

oil for frying

Sauce

½ cup vinegar

½ cup sugar

⅓ cup water

1 teaspoon salt

1 tablespoon sake

1 tablespoon soy sauce

2 shallots, chopped

*½ small capsicum (green pepper), cut into thin
strips*

few slices fresh ginger, shredded

Combine soy sauce and sake and marinate fish for 20 minutes. Remove and drain. Dust with
cornflour, heat oil in pan and fry until golden brown.

In the meantime, mix together sauce ingredients.

When fish is cooked, place on a serving dish and pour sauce over fish.

Pour boiling water over shallots and capsicum. Leave for 30 seconds, drain, and sprinkle
with ginger over the fish.

Serves 4

DAVID'S PICKLED MULLET

Thanks for this recipe to David Sinclair, who with his partner, John Morfesse, owns the Holiday Cottages at Goolwa in South Australia. David says that after a day's fishing the lowly mullet becomes a rare delight as the guests swap yarns about the one that got away. Never mind, he tells them. They'll come back next year and catch it — a kilo heavier!

1 kg (2 lb) mullet fillets, trimmed of little fins, etc.

1 litre (2 pints) white vinegar

7 heaped tablespoons sugar (or to taste)

2 heaped tablespoons cooking salt (or to taste)

2 onions, sliced

garlic

freshly ground pepper

handful chopped fresh dill

olive oil

Place mullet in salted water for about an hour.

Drain well, then place in a bowl and add vinegar in which sugar and salt have been dissolved.

Add onions, crushed garlic, lots of freshly ground pepper and a handful of chopped fresh dill. Mix well, then leave for a couple of days in the fridge.

Drain off liquid, pack into a jar with more sliced onion, and cover fish with olive oil. The fish are ready to eat after a few days.

MIRROR DORY IN CELERY SAUCE

Mirror (or silver) dory has now become quite popular, and when in season is an economical meal for all the family. Tim brought me some to try to work out a tasty dish, which I did. Lots of cooks would probably fry them like any other fillets of fish. I think they need slower cooking with ingredients that bring out the flavour. I do not and could not associate them with John Dory. The flesh and flavour is altogether different. John Dory is in a class all on its own, "super" class, but I must admit we all enjoyed this dish.

4–5 medium fillets (1 per person)

1 large can celery soup

milk

2 stalks celery

1 small onion, chopped finely

salt and freshly ground pepper

3 drops tabasco

½ teaspoon fresh or dry basil

1 tablespoon butter

1 tablespoon plain flour

1 tablespoon worcestershire sauce

strong cheese, grated

paprika

parsley, chopped

lemon wedges

Wash and dry fish and remove as many bones as possible.

Pour contents of can of soup into a large wide pan, wide enough to poach fish, not forgetting to add the same quantity of milk, as per directions on can. Add celery, onion and seasonings. Cook slowly for 15 minutes, add fish and poach for 10 minutes, taking care not to break fillets.

When cooked, remove fish from pan and place into flat baking dish. Leave celery sauce in pan ready to be thickened.

In saucepan, melt butter and add flour, stirring constantly. Add 1 cup milk and worcestershire sauce. When cooked and thickened, slowly stir into the celery sauce in which fish was poached, stirring all the time. Cook for a few minutes. Pour over fish in baking dish, sprinkle with cheese and brown under a hot griller, or in a hot oven.

When ready to serve, sprinkle with paprika and parsley. Garnish with lemon wedges and serve with potatoes that have been parboiled, drained, cut along the top, brushed with butter and browned under the griller. Some fairy toast also makes a nice accompaniment.

Fairy toast? You all know how to make that. I didn't once, so here is how. Bake some thin slices of bread in a hot oven until brown and crisp. You can store this toast for a while in an airtight container. Notice how every guest will keep nibbling at it and will finish up with more butter than toast.

Serves 4–5

MULLET SUPREME

2 large, beautiful, fat mullet

Marinade

2 cups white wine

1 cup brown vinegar

2 teaspoons peppercorns, crushed

juice of 1 large lemon

1 teaspoon salt

1 large brown onion, sliced

2 bay leaves, crumbled

pinch basil

Stuffing

2 cups cooked, fluffy rice, seasoned with salt and freshly ground pepper

1 brown onion, chopped

pinch nutmeg

pinch cinnamon

½ green and red capsicum (pepper), chopped finely

1 large stalk celery, chopped finely

½ cup plain flour

1 egg

1 cup milk

dash worcestershire sauce

dash tabasco sauce

1 clove garlic, crushed and sliced (optional)

oil or butter

Sauce

2 tablespoons butter or margarine

3 tablespoons plain flour

pinch salt and pepper

dash tabasco sauce

1 teaspoon mustard powder

2¼ cups milk or ½ milk, ½ fish stock

1 teaspoon anchovy paste or essence

paprika

parsley, chopped

lemon wedges

Ask your fishmonger to fillet the mullet, or take the whole mullet, remove head, cut away from backbone and remove. This lets the fish open flat.

Mix all marinade ingredients together and pour into a flat baking dish. (I like to use canned, green French peppercorns in this dish. I use them a lot in fish dishes, and they also make a nice addition to meat dishes. Pound them in a mortar or flatten them on a chopping board.) Place fish in dish and leave for 2 to 3 hours, turning fish as often as possible and spooning marinade over. When ready, drain off and discard marinade. Pat fish dry and remove black parts you may not have cleaned off. (Be careful with cooking after marinating, because the marinade partly "cooks" the fish.)

Mix together stuffing ingredients.

Grease a baking dish well with oil or butter. Flatten out mullet in dish and place some stuffing on each fish. Cover with well-greased foil and bake for 30 minutes in a hot oven.

To make sauce, melt butter in a saucepan over a low heat. Add flour and keep stirring until well combined. Add seasonings. (If you do not like sauce too hot, omit mustard.) Add milk slowly and keep stirring until you have a smooth, thick sauce (if too thick, add extra milk or cream). Add anchovy paste. This sauce can be used with any fish dish.

When fish is ready, remove foil and use egg slice to remove from baking dish. Pour over sauce, which must be very hot. Sprinkle with paprika and parsley and decorate with plenty of lemon wedges.

Practically any vegetable can be served with this dish, because the sauce will go with asparagus, cauliflower and also mashed potato, if liked—especially delicious is cooked celery.

Serves 6

ROLY POP FILLETS

salt and pepper
2½ teaspoons sugar
garlic salt (if liked)
1 brown onion, chopped
2 stalks celery, chopped
½ capsicum, chopped
tabasco sauce
½ teaspoon basil
juice of 2 large lemons

1 medium can whole tomatoes or 500 g (1 lb) ripe tomatoes
plain flour
4 large, beautifully cleaned, fat-free mullet fillets
2 teaspoons arrowroot
1 tablespoon brown vinegar or lemon juice
2 bay leaves
1 tablespoon chopped parsley
turkey skewers or toothpicks

Sprinkle baking dish with salt, pepper, 1 teaspoon sugar, and garlic salt, if used.

Combine onion, celery, capsicum, dash tabasco and basil. Sprinkle over lemon juice, and add half the tinned tomatoes and juice.

Flour fillets and roll and secure with skewers or whatever you have that will keep them in place—even string. Cover with lid or foil and bake in a preheated moderate oven.

Cook for 30 minutes—but, of course, you must always test fish to see if it is ready. If it flakes easily when tried with a fork, it is cooked.

Make a sauce of remaining tomatoes and juice, adding any extra juice from the fish. Put in a saucepan with arrowroot, remaining sugar, 2 drops tabasco, vinegar and bay leaves. Stir carefully, and when boiling, add parsley. Make sure arrowroot is cooked through.

Serve Roly Pop Fillets with sauce poured over and new potatoes garnished with parsley.

Serves 4

PILCHARDS MARINA

In Theo Roughley's *Fish and Fisheries of Australia* (a most interesting book for any keen fisherman), he wrote: "Much confusion exists in the public's mind concerning the relationship of the pilchard and sardine, and well it may, for the position is by no means clear. Originally the term 'sardine' was applied only to young pilchards and a valuable trade developed in south-western Europe, particularly in France and Portugal, canning them in oil."

Sardines or pilchards, they are delicious. This first recipe was given to me by the secretary to Graham Jones, former manager of the Sydney Fish Marketing Authority. He tells me that as well as being a great secretary, she is a great cook. After cooking Marina's pilchards, I heartily agree.

1 kg (2 lb) pilchards, heads and backbones removed
salt and pepper
plain flour
1 cup oil
2 large onions, sliced finely
1 clove garlic, crushed

few pieces lemon peel
1 bay leaf
1 teaspoon rosemary or ½ teaspoon powdered rosemary
½ cup white vinegar
¼ cup water

Season fish with salt and pepper and toss in flour, shaking off any excess.

Heat oil in pan until hot, add fish and fry until golden brown. When cooked, remove and arrange in casserole with lid.

Add ½ teaspoon flour to oil remaining in pan (if too much oil, discard some) and stir. Add onions and fry gently. Just before onions begin to colour, add garlic, lemon peel, bay leaf and rosemary, and stir.

Mix vinegar and water, add to pan, bring to boil and boil for a few minutes. Pour this marinade over fish and when cool, refrigerate for 24 hours, tossing occasionally.

NOTE: I made this as an entree for a small dinner party and served with it thin slices of bread baked in the oven until brown and crisp. It would be an ideal cold luncheon dish in summer with appropriate salads, especially lots of potato salad and hot garlic bread.

Serves 4

ALICE'S SARDINES

Sardines have a strong flavour, and after poaching them I leave them to cool, make some hot buttered toast, spread it with the sardines without breaking the little fillets, and top with lots of lemon juice, freshly ground pepper and a little salt if needed—simple and really good. I also like the dressing below.

2 kg (4 lb) fresh sardines, cleaned, with heads and backbones removed

water

salt

4 large bay leaves

4 sticks celery, chopped finely

12 black peppercorns, crushed

1 brown onion, chopped

½ lemon, chopped skin and all

On each side of backbone of sardine are fine, featherlike bones which should lift out with the backbone.

Put sardines carefully in a strainer and rinse under the tap, being careful not to break fillets. Place sardines in a large, heavy pan and cover with water. Add salt and remaining ingredients, slowly bring to boil, lower heat and simmer for 5 minutes. Cool in pan.

With a spatula or slotted spoon, gently remove sardines from pan and place in serving dish. Strain stock and reserve for use in a fish or oyster soup.

Simple Dressing for Sardines

1 clove garlic, crushed and chopped very finely

salt and freshly ground pepper

1 cup salad oil

½ teaspoon sugar

1 teaspoon salad herbs

2 tablespoons tarragon vinegar, or brown or white wine vinegar

Place garlic in bowl with pepper, salt and half the oil and mix gently. Add sugar and herbs, mix together again, add remaining oil and mix again. Finally add vinegar.

Place in a screwtop jar and shake a few times. Then, if you wish, season half the sardines you have cooked with this dressing. (Be careful not to break the little fillets and leave the cooked bay leaves on them.)

For the remaining sardines, use a simple dressing of pure olive oil, lemon juice, freshly ground pepper and salt and just a small amount of basil sprinkled over.

Serve sardines with piles of hot finger toast, and garnish with parsley and lemon wedges.

Sardines are also very nice made with the same recipe as for soused mullet (see page 138), but remember that, being small, they will cook very quickly.

SPANISH MACKEREL STUFFED WITH FRUIT

If you are fortunate enough to have some of this delicious fish from Australia's
Queensland coast, I think it should be given the champagne treatment. But first a
recipe for cooking whole mackerel. The mackerel I had was about 3.5 kg (7 lb)
before removing bones and head. Split mackerel (or you could use any large fish)
down the backbone and remove backbone and head. Leave tail on. This will open
up the fish ready to stuff.

Stuffing

*425 g (10 oz) can unsweetened apple or plum pulp
or 250 g (8 oz) cooked dried apricots (fruit
mixture should be fairly dry)*

1 egg yolk

½ cup sugar (omit if fruit is sweetened)

2 cups wholemeal or white breadcrumbs

juice of 1 lemon (optional)

1 teaspoon grated lemon rind (optional)

Mix stuffing ingredients together. Fill mackerel with stuffing, wrap in greased foil (coated with
olive oil for preference) and place in a preheated hot oven. Decrease heat and cook slowly in
a low oven for 45 minutes. (Test a couple of times to make sure you don't overcook it.)

Serves 6

SPANISH MACKEREL THE CHAMPAGNE WAY

*3.5 kg (7 lb) Spanish mackerel (or any large
  fish—kingfish, jewfish, etc.), filleted*

salt and freshly ground pepper

½ teaspoon basil

½ teaspoon dill

½ teaspoon fennel seeds

dry champagne

Sauce

90 g (3 oz) butter

1 tablespoon plain flour

salt and freshly ground pepper

2 drops tabasco sauce

2 cups milk

1 teaspoon mustard or anchovy essence (optional)

paprika

4 hard-boiled eggs, sliced

parsley

lemon wedges

celery

This dish may be served hot or cold.

Lay the mackerel fillets in a shallow dish and season with salt, pepper, basil, dill and fennel.
Pour the champagne over the fillets (the amount depending on how many fillets you have for
each person). Make sure the fish is well soaked.

Cover dish, place in a warm oven and simmer until cooked. Take care not to overcook
it as it will take only a short time (only about 20 minutes). If serving hot, place on serving plate,
decorate with parsley and lemon, and serve with sauce (below). If serving cold, turn off oven
and leave in oven until cold. Then turn out carefully on to a serving dish and refrigerate. When
ready to serve, decorate fish with plenty of parsley, lemons and crisp celery and serve with the
chilled sauce.

To make sauce, melt butter in a saucepan (be careful not to burn); add flour, salt, pepper
and tabasco. Using a wooden spoon, mix flour into hot butter and seasonings, until it is smooth.
Add milk very gradually and keep on stirring; do not let the mixture stick to the bottom of
the saucepan. Cook for a few minutes until raw flour taste has gone.

Add mustard or anchovy essence if liked. Mix well, pour into a serving jug, add eggs and
sprinkle with paprika. Serve hot or cold.

Serves 6

REDFISH FILLETS

Redfish are commonly known here as "Nannygai" (a lovely name—we all loved our Nannies). Select whole, fair-sized fish if possible, but if you like you can buy them already beautifully filleted direct from your friendly fishmonger—try to get them skinned, too. Remove bones if possible.

1 kg (2 lb) potatoes

1 onion, sliced

butter

milk

1 kg (2 lb) redfish fillets

salt and freshly ground pepper

parsley, chopped

juice of 1 lemon

breadcrumbs

Boil potatoes with onion, and when cooked strain well, making sure they are very dry. Mash with a little butter and milk.

Cut fish fillets in two if large. Place in a buttered frying pan and season with salt and pepper. Sprinkle with parsley and cover with some melted butter or margarine. Squeeze lemon juice over. Cover with buttered paper and fry gently for 5 to 7 minutes—no longer, please.

Remove fillets and drain on a piece of kitchen paper. (Do not place one fillet on top of another.)

Place redfish fillets in a heatproof dish, top with potato mixture, dot with butter and sprinkle with breadcrumbs and freshly ground pepper. Place under a hot griller to brown.

This dish is very good served with fresh green vegetables, such as zucchinis, or fried red or green capsicums, chopped firm tomatoes and celery pieces fried together in butter for 15 minutes only.

Serves 4

BAKED SNAPPER WITH TOMATOES

Thank you so much to George Andronicus (everybody knows Andronicus
coffee) both for this delicious recipe for snapper and for his help in putting this
book together. (If snapper is unobtainable, substitute any whole fish up to 1.5 kg
(3 lb) in weight.) George suggests his taramasalata (see page 35) as a good entree
to this main course dish.

1 kg (2 lb) snapper	*3 tablespoons flour*
2 cups chopped fresh tomatoes	*¼ cup cold water*
1 cup water	*3 teaspoons butter*
4 stalks celery, chopped	*salt*
2 teaspoons sugar	*paprika*
1 onion, sliced	*parsley*

Prepare fish for baking (see page 124) and place in a shallow baking dish. Put tomatoes, water,
celery, sugar and onion in saucepan and cook for 15 minutes.

Mix flour to a smooth paste with cold water. Melt butter in saucepan and stir in paste.
Add to the tomato mixture with salt and paprika.

Cook for another 10 minutes, then strain and pour over fish. Bake slowly in a warm oven
for about 45 minutes.

Serve on a hot platter garnished with parsley—with a green salad and grated zucchini.

Serves 4

SOLE IN CHAMPAGNE SAUCE

I am indebted to Mrs Monique Dircks-Dilly, wife of the former Consul-General of France, for this recipe, one of her favourites. Having made it, I have found for myself why Mrs Dircks-Dilly likes to serve it as a main dish for her husband and family as well as when entertaining (as they certainly must entertain a lot). I can imagine if this dish is served, guests will be clamouring to be invited again. When fillets of sole are unobtainable, other fish, of course, can be substituted. Please be careful of bones — it is best to bone the fish before marinating. If you have no champagne, use any sparkling cheaper wine or moselle.

6 fillets of sole or boned whiting
1 cup champagne
1 tablespoon lemon juice
salt and pepper
1 garlic clove, minced (optional)
300 ml (½ pint) pure cream

300 ml (½ pint) milk
parmesan cheese, freshly grated
250 g (½ lb) white seedless grapes
1 tablespoon chopped parsley
lemon slices

Marinate fillets for 30 minutes in champagne, lemon juice and seasonings. Remove and wrap in foil or parchment. Bake for 20 minutes in a moderate oven.

Make thin cream sauce by combining milk and cream and heating over low heat. (Do not boil.)

Unwrap fish and place on a heat-resistant platter. Pour cream sauce over, dust lightly with parmesan cheese and place grapes around fish. Brown lightly to golden colour under griller.

Garnish with parsley and lemon slices.

Serves 6

SUSAN RANICAR'S OCEAN TROUT
AND ATLANTIC SALMON

Trendy, tasty, terrific trout and succulent salmon—the "in" fish of the present day. By now, all fish lovers will have tasted the very popular ocean trout and Atlantic salmon. With their fine, tender flesh and beautiful deep-pink colour, they make a truly memorable meal.

I wasn't much used to eating trout because, living a lifetime on the beachfront at Watson's Bay, I had access to so much seafood. I thought of trout mainly in terms of sport-fishing. But three years ago, our son Peter took Jack and me for a trip to Tasmania to see one of the new trout farms. Well, it was new to me, at least—and fascinating. (Beautiful Tasmania, with its superb coastline, and what a charming city Hobart is—especially the area around Battery Point, which really takes you back to the days of the early settlers. Some great antique shops there, too.)

At Long Bay, Port Arthur, we visited a fish farm operated by Piers and Susan Ranicar and their family, owners of Tasmanian Smokehouse Pty Ltd. Here they farm both Atlantic salmon and ocean trout, and we saw how the fish are grown in floating net pens. The nets float in 12 to 15 metres of water, each pen holding about 5 tonnes of fish when the fish are fully grown. The fish are acclimatised to salt water by being exposed to gradually increasing degrees of salinity until they are ready to be transferred to the pens.

Back at the Ranicars' lovely home at Deloraine, we had the most delicious lunch. I felt I simply must include details of it here—my thanks to our charming hostess for generously responding to my request.

Amongst the appetising array of all foods bright and beautiful were round portions of smoked eel, served with fresh brown bread and butter and a delicious horseradish cream sauce (see page 158 for details). There were also platters of Atlantic salmon and fresh ocean trout, served cold—an ideal choice for those long, lazy summer days of outdoor eating. The sight of beautiful deep-pink salmon or trout lying on a big platter on a bed of fresh herbs, dill, parsley and coriander, garnished with slices of lemons or limes, is just superb. Here is Susie's recipe.

Stuff a whole salmon or trout with dill, parsley, lemon juice, a glass of white wine, salt and pepper, and half a clove of garlic, wrap in foil, and cook in the oven at 200°C (400°F) for about 30 minutes. Check during cooking, as it cooks very quickly. When cool, peel away the skin, and it's ready to eat. Serve with home-made mayonnaise.

Susan's Mayonnaise

2 egg yolks
salt
1 tablespoon white wine vinegar

2 teaspoons French mustard
about ¾ cup olive oil

Place first four ingredients in a food processor and mix for a few seconds. Very slowly, drip, then pour, olive oil into it, mixing all the while, and adding a tablespoon of hot water if it gets too thick.

RAINBOW TROUT

Rainbow trout are freshwater trout and, like most freshwater fish, not as flavoursome as the saltwater variety. They make very good eating nonetheless. This recipe was given to me by George Heydon.

1 whole rainbow trout, cleaned
salt and pepper
lemon juice

butter
bacon lard or dripping

Season fish with salt, pepper and lemon juice. Butter inside of fish and smear outside with bacon lard or dripping.

Wrap tightly in buttered foil. Bake in a moderate oven or under griller until cooked (about 30 minutes, according to size).

When ready, unwrap at table to retain flavour and juices.

Serves 2

TROUT AMANDINE

Thanks to Len Evans.

1 kg (2 lb) fillet of rainbow trout
salt and pepper
1 egg
1 cup milk
flour

½ cup butter
⅓ cup slivered almonds
juice of 2 lemons
2 tablespoons worcestershire sauce
1 tablespoon chopped parsley

Salt and pepper trout. Dip in batter of beaten egg and milk, then drain and dredge with flour.

In a heavy pan, melt butter and sauté trout for about 5 to 8 minutes, or until golden brown.

Remove trout to a warm platter.

Add almonds to pan and brown lightly. Add lemon juice, worcestershire sauce and parsley. Heat through and pour over fish.

Serves 3–4

PETER DOYLE JNR'S TROUT SCALLOP WITH GINGER, GARLIC AND TOMATOES

This dish is served by my grandson Peter at Doyle's on the Beach, Watson's Bay. It's a terrific recipe, as there is no need to cook the fish — the heat of the plate and the sauce cook it.

4 60 g (2 oz) slices ocean trout, skinned and boneless, not more than 5 mm (¼ in) thick
1 cup fish stock (page 41)
60 g (2 oz) piece ginger, peeled and finely chopped

3 cloves garlic, finely chopped
⅔ cup tomato concasse (skinned, peeled tomatoes, cut and drained; canned tomatoes can be used)
6 teaspoons butter

Preheat griller.

Pound trout slices until they are about 2 mm (⅛ in) thick. Pound from the centre outwards, taking care not to tear the flesh.

Mix fish stock, ginger, garlic and tomato concasse in a pan. Bring to boil and cook for 2 minutes. Keep hot on a low flame.

Spread 4 heat-resistant plates with ½ teaspoon melted butter each. Place plates under griller until hot.

Season fish with salt and pepper and place a piece on each plate.

Whisk remaining butter into sauce. Turn fish over on plates and pour sauce over. By the time you garnish the plates, the fish will be cooked.

Serves 4

SMOKED TROUT

Tim Doyle's favourite.

1 whole rainbow trout

Brine

1½ kg (3 lb) fine salt   *½ teaspoon pimento*
500 g (1 lb) white sugar   *½ teaspoon cardamom seeds*
1 teaspoon quick cure   *1 bay leaf*
30 g (1 oz) black pepper or crushed peppercorns   *11 litres (20 pints) water*
½ teaspoon allspice

Clean trout thoroughly, removing gills and point flaps. Combine brine ingredients and marinate trout for 48 hours. Hang overnight in smokebox (see page 126). Smoke for 8 hours.

To cook, poach in enough water to cover. When cooked, smother in butter and pepper and serve with lemon wedges. Taste before adding salt.

FRIED WHITEBAIT

Whitebait are tiny little fish—they say all good things come in small parcels. Well, these are good, but let's wrap them up in an airy-fairy flour seasoned with pepper and salt. Perhaps some kind friend will bring you some whitebait home, frozen, from New Zealand. Now and then we get some in Sydney. This recipe is for fresh whitebait.

whitebait   *salt and freshly ground pepper*
plain flour   *olive oil or other vegetable oil*

Make sure whitebait are free from sand and seaweed. Put into a wire mesh strainer and wash under a running tap. Dry well on a special, clean fine cloth you keep for fish only.

Place whitebait on a sheet of white butcher's paper on your workbench, and sprinkle lightly with flour seasoned with salt and pepper. Place whitebait in your wire chip-frying basket, place basket in deep oil and fry for about 5 minutes. Drain.

Sprinkle whitebait with lemon juice and freshly ground pepper.

Serve with thin fingers of brown bread and butter. Decorate with sprigs of parsley.

PAN-FRIED FRESH WHITING

My thanks to Jill Wran, the wife of the former New South Wales Premier, and a charming hostess, for this recipe. Whiting is a great fish for pan-frying, with its delicate flesh. The wholemeal flour gives it a nutty taste.

chillis, chopped	*wholemeal flour*
fresh herbs	*butter*
olive oil	*lemon juice*
6 medium, fresh whole whiting	*parsley*

Marinate chillis and herbs in olive oil.

Wash and clean whiting thoroughly. Dust with flour. (Place flour and fish together in a plastic bag and shake.)

Heat together in pan butter and olive oil in which herbs and chillis are marinating. Add whiting and fry, turning once and squeezing lemon juice on either side.

When golden brown and just cooked through (about 10 minutes), remove from pan and serve decorated with parsley.

Serves 6

ORIENTAL BARBECUED BREAM

This simple but delicious recipe was kindly supplied by Phil Nadin, General Manager of the New South Wales Fish Marketing Authority. He recommends sea bream as a good budget buy and finds fillets easier to barbecue than whole fish, as you can see how the fish is cooking.

750 g (1½ lb) sea bream fillets	*2 shallots, sliced*
¼ cup polyunsaturated oil	*1 clove garlic, crushed*
¼ cup soy sauce	*2 teaspoons chopped root ginger*
2 tablespoons sherry	

Combine oil, soy sauce, sherry, shallots, garlic and ginger. Mix until well combined.

Add bream fillets and allow to marinate for 1 to 2 hours. Drain; reserve marinade.

Place on a well-greased barbecue plate or grill. Cook for approximately 2 to 3 minutes each side, basting frequently with reserved marinade.

Serves 4-6

Menus

Here are some delicious dinner party menus featuring fish, kindly given to me by some well-known Australian hosts and hostesses. Thank you all.
*The asterisk indicates that the recipe follows.

FROM TAMIE FRASER

Figs Ricotta*
Fish with Herbs (see page 147)
Chocolate Pudding*

FIGS RICOTTA

Take 1 fresh fig, 1 tablespoon ricotta cheese, 2 slices prosciutto ham and 2 small slices canteloupe (rockmelon) per person.

Peel and slice the figs in half, fill with ricotta cheese and place decoratively on lettuce leaves, with the prosciutto and canteloupe.

Serve on individual plates.

CHOCOLATE PUDDING

6 eggs, separated
100 g (3½ oz) icing sugar
220 g (7 oz) cocoa
220 g (7 oz) butter

Cointreau or Benedictine
315 g (10 oz) chocolate meringues
whipped cream
grated chocolate

Mix egg yolks with 4 tablespoons icing sugar. Whisk well. Add cocoa, butter and rest of sugar, creamed together. Add a few spoons of Cointreau or Benedictine. Lastly, add well-whisked egg whites and fold in.

Line a mould with foil. Line sides and bottom with the meringues. Pour in some of the chocolate mixture, add a layer of meringues, followed by chocolate mixture, etc. Make about three or four layers. Chill in fridge an hour before serving. Garnish with whipped cream and a little grated chocolate.

PREVIOUS PAGE: The lifeboat was launched in 1870 as part of Rescue Services, which started that year. By 1900, the service was using self-righting rescue boats, as shown here.

FROM JILL WRAN,
WIFE OF THE FORMER NEW SOUTH WALES PREMIER

Curried Choko Soup*
Pan-fried Fresh Whiting (see page 189)
Baked Apples*

CURRIED CHOKO SOUP

4–6 chokos

olive oil

1 onion, chopped

1 teaspoon curry powder

2 chicken stock cubes

1½ cups water

salt to taste

Peel and seed chokos (I use rubber gloves to do this job), and slice into fairly thin slices. Brown slices in a little oil. (I always keep a jar of olive oil handy in which fresh herbs and chillis are marinating.)

Lift out choko slices (which you will have to brown in several batches) with a slotted spoon and transfer to a medium-sized saucepan.

Lightly brown onion in remaining oil. Stir in curry powder and cook a minute or two. Crumble in stock cubes.

Remove from heat, add water, stir, then pour over chokos. Simmer for about 10 minutes or until chokos are tender. Cool.

Blend in electric blender until smooth; season with salt if necessary. Reheat, adding more water if mixture is too thick, and serve.

BAKED APPLES

6 cooking apples

raisins or sultanas (optional)

60 g (2 oz) butter

cinnamon

2 tablespoons brown sugar

1 cup of white wine

1 tablespoon water

slivers of lemon rind

Wash and core apples. Pierce with a fork to prevent skins breaking. Stuff with raisins or sultanas if desired. Dot generously with butter and dust with cinnamon and sugar.

Mix the wine, water and lemon rind and pour over apples in a shallow baking dish.

Bake in a moderate oven for about 40 minutes or until they can be pierced with a skewer and are soft through.

Remove apples to serving dish, spoon sauce over each apple and serve with fresh cream.

FROM LEN EVANS

Watercress Soup*
Trout Amandine (see page 186)
Crepe Fitzgerald*
Assorted Australian Cheeses

WATERCRESS SOUP

1 cup butter	9 cups beef stock
1 large white onion, chopped	1 teaspoon salt
1 cup chopped celery, with a few leaves	½ teaspoon pepper
1 cup flour	1½ cups chopped watercress

Melt butter in a large saucepan. Sauté onion and celery until very tender. Stir in flour and continue cooking over low heat for 8 to 10 minutes, stirring constantly. Blend in beef stock, salt and pepper. Simmer for 30 minutes. Stir in watercress.

Makes just over 2 litres (2 quarts)

CREPE FITZGERALD

2 crepes	sugar
2 heaped teaspoons Philadelphia cream cheese	butter
2 tablespoons sour cream	strawberry liqueur
½ cup strawberries	kirsch

Roll cream cheese and sour cream in crepes and put on a plate. In a chafing dish, cook strawberries in sugar and butter. Flame in strawberry liqueur and kirsch, and pour over crepes.

Serves 1

BEAUTIFUL WHOLE BAKED SNAPPER *(PAGE 124)*

FLO AND ALICE'S SPECIAL FISH DISH *(PAGE 149)*

DINNER ON THE P&O LINER
SEA PRINCESS

Danish Caviar
Cream of Asparagus Soup
Prawns Provençale
(cooked with tomatoes, parsley, shallots, garlic, capers, olives
and anchovy fillets, served with risotto)
Prime Fillet of Beef Wellington
with braised celery hearts
and sauté potatoes
Lemon Gâteau

DINNER AT DAGNINO'S

We had this superb dinner in the private dining room of Captain Dagnino, Master of the Sitmar liner *Fairstar*. We enjoyed the food and the company as the ship glided over the China Sea, a full moon reflecting its beauty on a vast ocean.

Smoked Salmon alla Parisienne
Italian Hors d'Oeuvres
Lobster Tail alla Thermidor
(crayfish tail with cream sauce, grated cheese topping,
browned under griller)
Baked Prime Ribs al Sale with Bearnaise Sauce
with jacket potatoes and corn on the cob
Soufflé au Grand Marnier

FROM MARGARET WHITLAM

Oyster Soup
or
Prawns with Mayonnaise
Baked Seasoned Barramundi
with potatoes baked in their jackets
and crisp salad of lettuce, cucumber and nuts
Sliced Fresh Pineapple
Cheese Platter

FROM ELSA JACOBY, MBE

A family Good Friday meal (Serves 5)

Toheroa Soup (see page 40)
Smoked Haddock with Poached Eggs (see page 168)
Peaches in Red Wine*

PEACHES IN RED WINE

Simmer 5 peeled fresh peaches in about ¾ cup water and sugar to taste for about 15 minutes, turning occasionally. Add a large cup red wine and simmer until wine has evaporated and syrup thickened. Cool a little. Serve peaches with vanilla ice-cream, with a little syrup poured over.

FROM FORMER MATRON YORK
OF ST LUKE'S HOSPITAL

Australian Avocado and Prawns (see page 74)
Pan-fried Fish (see page 123)
with Herbed Tomato Sauce*
creamy buttered mashed potatoes
and hot bread rolls
Strawberries
marinated in cherry brandy
and topped with sugar

HERBED TOMATO SAUCE

6 canned tomatoes, drained and chopped finely	*1 bay leaf, crumbled*
30 g (1 oz) butter	*pinch dill*
2 large onions, chopped finely	*pinch basil*
2 stalks celery, chopped finely	*3 drops tabasco*
1 teaspoon sugar	*salt and freshly ground pepper*

Place all ingredients in a saucepan; cook, covered, until onion and celery are tender. Serve on the side of the fish.

Sailing at Sydney Heads at the turn of the century.

FROM HAZEL HAWKE,
WIFE OF THE HONOURABLE R. J. HAWKE,
PRIME MINISTER OF AUSTRALIA

Spring Vegetable Soup
Sate Prawns*
with a mixed green salad
Fruit Salad in Chocolate Baskets*

SATE PRAWNS

750 g (1 lb) shelled green prawns

2 tablespoons oil

3 small onions, cut into wedges

roughly chopped lettuce

Marinade

2 tablespoons sate sauce

½ teaspoon five spice powder

pinch sugar

pinch salt

chilli sauce to liking

1 teaspoon cornflour

1 teaspoon soy sauce

1 nip dry sherry

Blend marinade ingredients in a bowl. Add deveined prawns, mix well and stand for 2 hours.

Heat oil in pan, add onion wedges and sauté briskly for 2 minutes. Add prawns and marinade and cook for a further 4 to 5 minutes. Place a tablespoon or two of water in the empty marinade bowl, swirl around and add to pan, if needed. On your serving plate put a layer of crisp, roughly chopped lettuce (or rice or wild rice) and dish prawns over. Serve immediately.

FRUIT SALAD IN CHOCOLATE BASKETS

All the fruit must be absolutely fresh — nothing canned! Sweeten to your liking. If the fruits are on the bland side (as in winter), add some cognac or kirsch half an hour before serving.

Fill the chocolate baskets with fruit and decorate with a rosette of whipped cream topped with a strawberry.

To make individual chocolate baskets, melt plain dark chocolate to 37°C. For each basket, spread on a piece of greaseproof paper, with a palette knife, a circle of chocolate 120 mm (4 ½ in) diameter, 1 mm thick. Place paper on an upturned glass. Place glass and chocolate-covered paper in refrigerator. After 24 hours remove paper. Freeze baskets until ready to use.

FROM KATHRYN GREINER,
WIFE OF THE NEW SOUTH WALES PREMIER

Platter of Oysters, Prawns, Crabs and Smoked Eel
served with lemon and garnished with watercress
Barbecue Fish*
Chocolate Soufflé

BARBECUE FISH

catch of the day (jewfish cutlets are a favourite
    of the Greiners)

lemon juice

soya sauce

2 tablespoons butter

Place fish in centre of a greased sheet of foil with butter, lemon juice and soya sauce.
    Wrap fish envelope-style and place on barbecue. (Get your favourite man to cook it!)
    A crisp white wine is a good accompaniment.

FROM GEORGE ANDRONICUS

Taramasalata (see page 35)
with bread or crisp raw vegetables
Fried Whitebait (see page 188)
Baked Snapper with Tomatoes (see page 183)
Pineapple Sorbet
Coffee
(Andronicus, of course! A.D.)

Doyle's Fish Cookbook

FROM JANETTE HOWARD

Dinner Party Menu for 8

Baked Oysters Bluevein*
Mediterranean Stuffed Fish*
Fresh Berries in Curacao*

BAKED OYSTERS BLUE VEIN

4 dozen oysters on shell, or 1 bottle 50 oysters, drained (6 oysters per head)
¼ cup sour light cream
½ teaspoon tabasco sauce
3 tablespoons fresh basil, finely chopped
1 tablespoon fresh lemon juice

1 cup fresh wholemeal breadcrumbs
2 cloves garlic, crushed
1 tablespoon butter or margarine
2 tablespoons blue vein cheese, grated
freshly ground black pepper

Combine in a bowl sour cream, tabasco, basil and lemon juice. Mix well.

Arrange opened oysters on an oven slide, or, if using bottled oysters, divide between 4 ovenproof dishes.

Melt butter or margarine in a saucepan, add breadcrumbs and garlic, and stir until crisp and golden. Remove from heat and add blue vein cheese and pepper.

Spoon the basil sour cream evenly over the oysters and top with the cheese crumb mixture. Bake at 200°C (about 400°F) for 12 minutes.

MEDITERRANEAN STUFFED FISH

8 whole silver bream, scaled and gutted
3 cups fresh wholegrain breadcrumbs
3 tablespoons lemon juice
1 cup fresh orange juice
4 tablespoons pine nuts

6 tablespoons currants
½ teaspoon ground oregano
freshly ground black pepper
2 teaspoons butter or margarine
juice of 2 lemons

Combine breadcrumbs, lemon and orange juice and mix well. Add pine nuts, currants, oregano and pepper.

Melt butter or margarine in frypan and fry stuffing until lightly browned. Remove from heat. Fill each fish cavity with stuffing, packing in firmly, and secure with toothpicks.

Lightly grease 8 pieces of foil with oil. Place fish on foil, sprinkle with black pepper and lemon juice. Cover and seal edges to form envelope. Place on baking slide and bake at 180°C (350°F) for 15 to 20 minutes. Serve with an assortment of vegetables.

200

FRESH BERRIES IN CURACAO

Simply marinate seasonal berries in curacao and serve with clotted cream.

FROM SENATOR JANINE HAINES,
LEADER OF THE AUSTRALIAN DEMOCRATS

Crab Bisque*
Individual Beef Wellingtons
with madeira sauce and vegetables in season
Fresh Seasonal Fruit
soaked overnight in Grand Marnier and served with chantilly cream

CRAB BISQUE

4 blue swimmer crabs, uncooked	*¼ cup uncooked white rice*
8 cups water	*2 teaspoons tomato paste*
1 onion, chopped	*2 egg yolks, beaten*
60 g (2 oz) butter	*½ cup cream*
½ cup dry white wine	*1 or 2 tablespoons fresh dill*
¼ cup brandy	*freshly ground black pepper*
2 medium tomatoes, peeled and chopped	*sour cream (optional)*

Remove meat from crab shells, discarding any grey tissue.

Place washed shells in a large saucepan with 8 cups water. Bring to boil and simmer, uncovered, for 30 minutes. Strain and reserve stock. (Discard the shells well away from the neighbourhood cats!)

Cook chopped onion in butter in a large saucepan. When onion is soft, add wine, brandy and stock. Bring to boil and add chopped tomatoes, rice and tomato paste. Simmer, uncovered, for 20 minutes.

Combine beaten egg yolks with cream and add to soup. Blend to a smooth consistency. Add chopped crab meat, fresh dill and some freshly ground black pepper. Reheat, but do not boil.

Serve with a "blob" of sour cream if desired.

Serves 6

FROM LYNNE ALLEN-BROWN,
MATRON OF ST LUKE'S HOSPITAL, SYDNEY

Dinner Party Menu for 8

**Small cocktail toasts with avocado and caviar,
black olive paste and cherry tomato*
Iced Gazpacho*
served with fairy toast (see page 175)
Poached Ocean Trout*
with hollandaise sauce (see page 70), new potatoes with chives, green beans al dente and (if desired)
hot rolls with butter
Mango Meringue Torte with Berries*
Bavarian Blue Cheese with Crackers**

BLACK OLIVE PASTE

2 dozen black olives, stoned
½ clove garlic

2 teaspoons olive oil

Blend to a paste, spread on little cocktail toasts, and top with half a cherry tomato and a sprig of basil.

AVOCADO PASTE

1 ripe avocado, mashed
½ onion, grated or very finely chopped

2 teaspoons lemon juice
salt and pepper to taste

Mash ingredients together, spread on little cocktail toasts, and top with ¼ teaspoon black lumpfish caviar and a tiny segment of sliced lemon.

GAZPACHO

1 large can tomato juice

1 can beef consomme

1 large can peeled tomatoes plus juice

4 tablespoons tomato paste

1 onion, chopped

½ cucumber, peeled and seeded

½ green capsicum, chopped

½ cup cooked peas

1 slice white bread, crusts removed, soaked
  in ¼ cup olive oil with dash white vinegar

1 clove garlic

freshly ground pepper

salt to taste

good dash tabasco and/or chilli sauce

Blend all ingredients until liquid, and strain if desired. Chill very well. Serve cold with side dishes of (additional) chopped capsicum, tomato, shallots and seeded cucumber, and fairy toast or crackers.

POACHED OCEAN TROUT

1 large ocean trout (about 1.5 kg or 3 lb)

125 g (4 oz) butter

3 lemons

parsley

Wash trout in cold water.

Grease a large sheet of foil with butter, place fish in centre of foil, and place sliced lemon around, over and in fish (about 2 lemons).

Slice about 125 g butter and put over and in fish.

Wrap like a parcel, and place in another piece of foil. Bake in a moderate oven for 20 to 25 minutes, or until cooked. (Do not overcook.)

Serve on a large platter, decorated with parsley and lemon wedges.

If serving with hollandaise sauce, be sparing, so that the sauce does not overpower the delicacy of the fish.

MANGO MERINGUE TORTE WITH BERRIES

2 dinner-plate-sized meringue shells

2 large fresh mangoes, sliced

1 punnet cream

1 punnet strawberries

1 punnet raspberries

1 punnet blueberries

Just before serving, join meringue shells together with the sliced mango and whipped cream.

Cut and serve on an entree plate, with 1 or 2 tablespoons mixed berries.

FROM LUCILA MADDOX,
DIETITIAN AT ST LUKE'S HOSPITAL, SYDNEY

A low-fat, low-cholesterol menu for 10

Melon Frappé*
Pickled Fish*
Fruit Crepes*

MELON FRAPPÉ

3 medium-sized rockmelons

1 cup sherry or brandy

½ cup lemon juice

1 teaspoon salt

1 cup grated walnuts (2 teaspoons per serve)

crushed ice

Cut rockmelons in quarters. (You'll have half a melon to spare.) Remove seeds, and make incisions lengthwise and crosswise (as though dicing, but without cutting right through). Place in individual bowls.

Mix together sherry or brandy, lemon juice and salt, and spoon over melon quarters. Sprinkle with grated walnuts (2 teaspoons per serve) and garnish, if desired, with mint and/or cherries. Serve very cold on a bed of crushed ice.

PICKLED FISH

10 fillets fish (snapper, bream, jewfish), boned

3 cloves garlic, crushed

10 tablespoons fine carrot strips

5 tablespoons fine onion strips

2 tablespoons fine leek strips

1 tablespoon fine capsicum strips

2 tablespoons fine celery strips

2½ tablespoons polyunsaturated oil

1 bay leaf

2 or 3 cloves

2 tablespoons lemon juice

1 tablespoon dry white wine

1 tablespoon white vinegar

1 teaspoon cumin

2 teaspoons coriander

½ teaspoon freshly ground black pepper

1 cup water

orange slices and parsley to garnish

2 tablespoons (50 g) gelatine dissolved in 250 ml water (for cold version only)

Brown garlic lightly in oil. Add vegetable strips, bay leaf, cloves, cumin, coriander, pepper and water, and cook for 10 to 15 minutes until tender.

Add lemon juice, wine and vinegar. Simmer for another 5 minutes.

Place fish fillets in a large baking dish and cover with the cooked vegetable pickle. Cook for 10 minutes in a hot oven, or cover and cook over a low heat on top of stove for 10 to 15 minutes.

Serve hot or cold (see below), garnished with orange slices and parsley. New potatoes and champignons are a good accompaniment.

If serving cold, add gelatine mixture at end of cooking time, allow to cool and refrigerate.

FRUIT CREPES

Batter

4 eggs, separated
250 g (8 oz) plain flour, sifted
2 cups low-fat or skimmed milk
1 cup low-fat cottage cheese
2 tablespoons brandy or rum

pinch sugar
pinch nutmeg
pinch salt
few drops vanilla essence
2 tablespoons polyunsaturated margarine for cooking

Filling

fruit in season, sliced

skim milk/ricotta mixture, non-fat plain or fruit yoghurt, or buttermilk (see method)

Beat egg yolks with remaining batter ingredients (except margarine) until mixture is combined and smooth. Beat egg whites until they form firm peaks. Fold into batter.

Drop spoonfuls into a lightly greased pan, shake pan to spread, brown lightly and flip.

For filling, mix sliced fruit of your choice (such as peaches, plums and strawberries — about 2 tablespoons per serve) with one of the following: mixture of 1 part skim or evaporated skim milk to 2 parts low-fat ricotta cheese; non-fat yoghurt; or buttermilk. Spread with a little sugar.

Fill crepes with fruit mixture and fold. Serve topped with a little extra sliced fruit an extra spoonful of the milk mixture, and garnished with mint leaves.

FROM DON FRANCOIS,
FORMER DIRECTOR OF FISHERIES, NEW SOUTH WALES STATE FISHERIES

Oysters au Naturel (see page 99)
Baked Flathead with Ham (see page 162)
with crisp green salad
Fresh Fruit Salad
or
Iced Grapes and Melon

ALICE DOYLE'S MENU
FOR ANY DAY OF THE WEEK

Breakfast
1 fresh whole grapefruit

sardines on toast (see page 179)

toast, marmalade and tea

11 am *coffee and cake*

Lunch
Bonzer fish and chips

fresh bread rolls

cup of tea

3 pm *coffee and biscuit*

Dinner
Bonzer fish and chips

and, if lucky, a few prawns

glass of Doyle's riesling

Midnight *oil—I burn it up.*

Of course we eat fish—we have to, especially on Monday (what's left over in the restaurants from the weekend). Don't pity us. Name a better source of protein. No butchers' answers please!

Buying & Keeping Fish

The following information was kindly provided by the Sydney Fish Marketing Authority, Pyrmont.

How Much to Buy?

Whole fish 900 g–1 kg (2–2¼ lb) Serves 2

Whole fish, gutted, with head, fins and tail removed 450 g–500 g (about 1 lb) Serves 2

Steaks or cutlets 500 g (1 lb) Serves 2–3

Skinned fillets 500 g (1 lb) Serves 3–4

Guide to Quality

Fresh whole fish have bright, full eyes and gills that are red and free from disagreeably smelly slime. The flesh is elastic, springing back when gently pressed. There should be a mild characteristic odour.

How Long to Keep

Fresh fish should be used as soon as possible after purchase. It will remain in good condition for up to 15 days when packed in flake ice, but at the cabinet temperature of a refrigerator (about 4°–5°C) it is edible for up to 3 days and bad after 6. Keep fish on a plate covered with waxed paper, foil or plastic in the coldest part of the refrigerator.

Frozen Fish

Domestic freezers (–18° to –23°C) should not be used to store fish for longer than 3 months. The temperature of a refrigerator ice box is –7° to –12°C. Do not store fish in ice boxes for more than a week.

Once frozen fish is thawed, it deteriorates at a faster rate than fresh fish, so use immediately. Never re-freeze thawed fish.

Breaded fish—scallops, fish fingers and fillets—should never be thawed before cooking.

PREVIOUS PAGE: The old Vaucluse Council's workyards at Watson's Bay.

AVAILABILITY: WHEN AND WHERE

Variety	NT	Qld	NSW	Vic	Tas	SA	WA
Barramundi (*giant perch*)	**	Nov-Mar	—	—	—	—	Apl-Nov
Bream, black	—	Jne	**	**	—	—	**
Bream, silver	—	—	May-Jne	—	—	—	—
Cod, Murray	—	—	**	Jan-Oct	—	Dec-Aug	—
Crab, mud	**	Feb-Apl	Nov-Feb	—	—	—	**
Crab, sand	—	Nov-Mar	**	—	—	—	Jan-Mar
Flathead, river (*black*)	—	May-Jly	**	**	—	—	Jan-Aug
Flathead, sand	—	May-Jly	Jan-Mar	**	**	**	—
Flathead, tiger	—	—	Jan-Mar	**	**	—	—
Gemfish							
(*hake, king barracouta*)	—	—	Jly-Aug	Mar-Jne	—	—	—
Jewfish (*mulloway*)	**	Apl-May	Mar-Apl	—	—	Nov-May	Aug-Apl
Jewfish, Westralian (*dhu*)	—	—	—	—	—	—	**
John Dory	—	*	Feb-Apl	*	**	—	—
Kingfish, yellowtail	—	Jne	Jan-Mar	**	—	Jan-Mar	—
Leatherjacket, ocean	—	—	Feb-Apl	**	**	**	**
Leatherjacket,							
rough (*yellow*)	—	—	**	—	—	**	Mar-Jne
Lobster, rock	—	—	Jly-Aug	**	Nov-Aug	Nov-Sep	Nov-Aug
Mackerel, Spanish	**	Oct-Dec	**	—	—	—	Jly-Oct
Morwong (*sea bream*)	—	—	Apl-Jly	**	**	—	Dec-Aug
Mullet	—	Apl-Jly	Feb-Apl	**	**	**	Jan-Mar
Oysters, Sydney rock	—	**	**	**	—	—	Apl-Nov
Perch, pearl	—	Apl-Jly	**	—	—	—	—
Prawns, banana	—	Feb-Jne	—	—	—	—	—
Pranws, bay	—	Dec-Apl	—	—	—	—	—
Prawns, king	Jne-Dec	Nov-Sep	**	**	—	**	Mar-Sep
Prawns, school	—	Feb-Apl	Nov-Mar	**	—	—	Dec-Apl
Prawns, tiger	—	May-Sep	—	—	—	—	—
Redfish (*nannygai*)	—	—	May-Jne	**	—	—	Dec-Aug
Red emperor	—	Mar-Jly	—	—	—	—	—
Red sweetlip	—	Mar-Jly	—	—	—	—	—
Salmon, Australian	—	—	**	**	**	**	Feb-May
Scallops, sea	—	Sep-Mar	*	**	May-Nov	May-Jly	Mar-Sep
Shark (*flake*)	**	*	**	**	**	**	Feb-Sep
Snapper	—	Apl-Jly	May-Jne	**	—	**	Apl-Sep
Squid	Jne-Dec	Feb-Apl	**	**	Nov-Feb	**	**
Trevally	**	*	**	**	**	—	Feb-Jly
Trout, coral	—	Mar-Jly	—	—	—	—	—
Tuna	—	Feb-May	**	May-Jne	Jan-Jun	Jan-Apl	Feb-Aug
Whiting, sand	—	May-Aug	**	**	—	—	Jly-Nov
Whiting, King George	—	—	**	**	**	**	Mar-Aug

**available all year   *available occasionally or in small quantities   — not available

SOME POPULAR TABLE FISH

Barramundi or giant perch
Considered by many to be Australia's top eating fish because of its moist, flavoursome, well-textured flesh. Many lesser species are sometimes misrepresented as barramundi.

Bream
A delicate table fish, usually bought in small fillets.

Coral trout and cod
These two magnificent table fish, occasionally confused with each other, compete for the honour of premium fish of the Great Barrier Reef.

Crayfish
Also called rock lobster. It is considered a gastronomic delight the world over. The flesh is white, firm and sweet, with a distinctive flavour all its own.

Flathead
The flesh of the tiger flathead is white, tender and flavoursome. It never reaches a size that makes it coarse or tough as some other flathead species sometimes do. The river flathead ranks high as a food fish. Although the flesh is a little dry, it is white, firm and has a good flavour. The sand flathead is similar in taste and texture to the tiger.

Gemfish, hake or king barracouta
A fish of excellent quality with a good-textured flesh. It has a pleasant though slightly more pronounced flavour than most Australian fish. A tasty smoked product has been developed.

Morwong or sea bream
A good eating fish similar to bream but a little stronger in flavour.

Jewfish or mulloway
Young jewfish of 1–3 kg are excellent eating. In fish below the length of 46 cm, the flesh tends to be soft and mushy. The flesh of large mulloway becomes flaky, with a tendency to coarseness and loss of flavour.

John Dory
Considered a delicacy of the sea. A prominent black spot on each side is said to represent the imprints of St Peter's thumb and first finger, made as he took a piece of money from the fish's mouth. The flesh is firm, white and tender, with a deliciously succulent flavour.

Leatherjacket
Good eating fish with delicate white flesh. Best cooked whole.

Mirror dory or silver dory
A tasty fish with firm, white flesh. Usually an economical buy.

Mullet
A much-maligned fish because it occasionally has an "earthy" flavour. If prepared and cooked correctly, this is a fish of exceptionally good quality. The flavour is rich and the flesh always tender, except for a short period after spawning when the flesh darkens.

Murray cod
A gourmet's delight and the most delicious of Australia's inland freshwater fish. It has white, firm flesh of good quality, and can be cooked in many ways.